CHATGPT4 SIMPLE 2 D GAME LAZARUS(PASCAL) PROGRAMMING

STEP BY STEP GAME DEVELOPMENT APPROACH WITH APPENDIX OF PASCAL GRAMMER AND LAZARUS DETAIL

MOONWOLF

Copyright Notice

Special Recommendation for Educational Use

As the author of this book, I strongly recommend "ChatGPT4 Simple 2D Game Lazarus(Pascal) programming" as an essential reference material for educators, students, and anyone embarking on the journey of learning programming. This book is particularly suited for:

Programming Educators:

Whether you're teaching high school students, college undergraduates, or adult learners, this book offers a comprehensive guide to understanding and applying the concepts of Pascal programming and game development in Lazarus. It can serve as a textbook, a supplementary resource, or a guide for creating curriculum content.

Programming Beginners:

If you are just starting out in the world of programming, this book is designed with you in mind.

It breaks down complex concepts into understandable segments, guiding you through each step of creating a 2D game and understanding the fundamentals of Pascal and Lazarus.

Self-Learners and Hobbyists:

For those who are teaching themselves programming and game development, this book offers a structured approach to learning, ensuring that you build a solid foundation of skills.

While this book is copyrighted material, I encourage its use in educational settings as a reference to enhance the learning experience.

It is my hope that this book will not only impart knowledge but also inspire a passion for programming and game development.

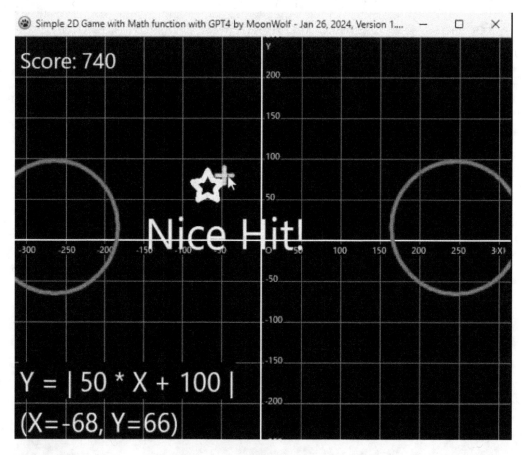

This is the Game what we are going to be discussed in this book. A Star moves left to right by Mathematical functions. Users aim the moving star by clicking the mouse. There is a small-time lag between the clicking and the bullet reach the point. So, you need to shoot the star location when 0.5 second later.

The sample movie can be checked here:

https://twitter.com/MoonWolf_Eng/status/175222514345854999
74

Welcome to the World of Lazarus and Pascal Programming

Have you ever dreamed of creating your own Windows applications or games but felt overwhelmed by complex programming languages like C?

This book is your gateway into the fascinating world of software development, tailored specifically for beginners.

I introduce you to Lazarus, a user-friendly environment perfect for those taking their first steps in programming.

It's based on the Pascal language, known for its simplicity and clarity, making it an ideal starting point for aspiring developers.

Why Lazarus and Pascal?

Ease of Learning:

Unlike C language, which can be daunting for beginners due to its complexity, Lazarus and Pascal offer a more approachable learning curve.

Their straightforward syntax and structure make understanding and writing code much easier.

Powerful, Yet Simple:

While Lazarus is simple enough for beginners, it's also powerful. It allows you to create from full-fledged Windows applications to developing operating systems or hardware drivers.

Cross-Platform Compatibility:

Though our focus is on Windows, Lazarus isn't limited to it. It also supports MacOS and Linux, offering flexibility and a wide range of possibilities.

More Than Just a Game: An Introduction to Mathematics

This book isn't just about building a game.
It's an exploration of mathematical functions and their visualization.

Programming With a Twist: The ChatGPT-4 Companion

Embrace a new era of coding where you're not alone. ChatGPT-4, an advanced AI, will be your guide and companion throughout this journey.

Whether you're stuck with a bug or need creative solutions, ChatGPT-4 is here to assist, making the learning process interactive and efficient.

For The Budding Developers

If you're a high school student with a curiosity for technology, this book is for you. It's crafted to help you understand the basics of programming and game development, blending learning with fun and creativity.

By the end of this book, not only will you have a solid foundation in Lazarus and Pascal, but you'll also have a deeper appreciation for how programming can bring mathematics to life in fun and interactive ways.

Your Journey Begins Here

As you turn each page, you'll find yourself growing more confident in your programming skills.

With ChatGPT-4 by your side and a focus on practical, enjoyable learning, you're about to embark on an exciting journey into the world of programming.

What else is important beside of programming?

As we conclude this introduction, it's particularly important for younger readers, especially if you are a middle or high school student, to understand a key aspect of personal and professional development.

While proficiency in programming is a valuable skill, it alone may not be enough to excel in the wider world.

To truly thrive in society, it's essential to cultivate a range of interpersonal and soft skills alongside your technical abilities.

These include communication skills, persuasiveness, foresight, negotiation skills, ethical understanding, the ability to discern the essence of issues, awareness of global events, imagination, creativity, empathy to understand what people need and desire, patience, perseverance, cross-cultural understanding, and the ability to engage in intercultural exchanges.

By developing these skills in tandem with your programming abilities, you'll not only enhance your technical proficiency but also turn it into one of your most attractive qualities.

This holistic approach to learning will prepare you to navigate the complexities of the world and make a significant impact in your future endeavors.

Now, are you ready to take your first step into the realm of software development? Let's get started!

*** This book is written by MoonWolf in English assisted by ChatGPT4 to give you clear and natural English.

Dear Readers,

Welcome to your journey into the world of programming with Lazarus. Before you begin, I would like to share some important points regarding the support and responsibilities related to this book:

1.   Windows Knowledge and Lazarus Installation:

This book assumes a basic understanding of the Windows operating system. It does not cover the installation process of Lazarus in detail. For installation guidance, please refer to external sources or the official Lazarus documentation.

2.   Limitation of Support:

As the author, MoonWolf, I do not provide personal support for questions related to Lazarus, its installation, errors that may occur, or any other related technical issues. This includes troubleshooting, debugging, or resolving specific challenges you might encounter while using Lazarus.

3.   Encouragement for Self-Research:

I strongly encourage you to actively engage in the learning process. Researching, experimenting, and solving problems on your own are key components of mastering programming skills.

4.   Disclaimer of Liability:

I, MoonWolf, cannot be held responsible for any direct, indirect, incidental, or consequential damages resulting from the use of information contained in this book, or from the use of programs and source code that may accompany it. This includes, but is not limited to, damages or issues arising from the installation or use of Lazarus, any PC troubles, or any other outcomes related to the contents of this book.

This book is intended to guide and educate you through the basics of game development with Lazarus. It aims to inspire creativity and independent problem-solving skills.

However, it is your responsibility to ensure that your use of Lazarus and any related software does not adversely affect your system.

Thank you for choosing this book as your companion on this exciting journey. I wish you an enriching and enjoyable learning experience.

Best regards,

MoonWolf

Contents

11

Document change history

DATE	Document Version	Remarks
2024.Jan.31	Kindle 1.00	First Kindle version release
2023.Feb.01	Kindle 1.00 PPB 0.50	First Paperback release

In this chapter, you will know below:

[1] What is PASCAL

[2] What is Lazarus

[3] How to install Lazarus

[4] Practice first step program

Pascal is a high-level programming language, which means it's designed to be easy for humans to read and write.

Think of it like giving instructions to a robot. Just as you might write a recipe with steps for cooking a dish, programming in Pascal involves writing instructions for the computer to follow.

These instructions are written in a way that both the computer and a human can understand.

A Brief History of Pascal

Pascal was developed in the late 1960s by a Swiss computer scientist named Niklaus Wirth. The language is named after the French mathematician and philosopher Blaise Pascal.

Wirth created Pascal to encourage good programming practices involving structured programming and data structuring.

Originally, Pascal was designed as a tool for teaching programming, but it quickly gained popularity for its simplicity and effectiveness in software development.

C Language:

Complexity:

C is a powerful language used in system programming and developing operating systems. Its syntax can be more complex and less intuitive for beginners.

Flexibility and Control:

C offers greater control, which is crucial in system-level programming. However, this can be overwhelming for new programmers.

Pointers and Memory Management:

C requires a deep understanding of pointers and memory management, which can be challenging for beginners.

Popularity in Industry:

C is widely used in professional environments, especially for system and application development, making it a valuable skill for a career in software development.

Programming language Pascal:

Simplicity and Clarity:

Pascal is designed to be simple and readable. Its syntax is straightforward, making it easier for beginners to understand and learn.

Structured Programming:

Pascal encourages structured programming practices, helping beginners develop a clear programming mindset.

Error Checking:

Strong type checking in Pascal helps catch errors early in the learning process, making debugging simpler.

Educational Tool:

Pascal is often used as an educational tool to teach the fundamentals of programming, focusing on concepts over complex syntax.

Why Pascal is Good for Beginners and Students

Ease of Learning:

Pascal's clear and structured syntax makes it an ideal starting point for beginners and students new to programming.

Foundation for Advanced Concepts:

Learning Pascal provides a solid foundation in programming logic and structured design, which are essential skills in any programming language.

Transition to Complex Languages:

The experience gained from learning Pascal can be a stepping stone to more complex languages like C.

Understanding the basics in a simpler language makes the transition to a more complex language smoother.

Focus on Programming Concepts:

Since Pascal is less about syntax complexity and more about programming concepts, it allows students to focus on learning the core principles of programming.

Pascal's Capability in Windows Application Development
While C is popular in professional environments, Pascal also possesses the capability to develop robust Windows applications.

Lazarus, an IDE for Pascal, is particularly effective for this purpose.

Pascal's clear syntax and strong error checking make it a suitable choice for developing Windows applications, especially for those who have started their programming journey.

For students and beginners who are more comfortable with Pascal, leveraging its potential to create Windows applications can be both educational and practical.

The skills and logic developed while programming in Pascal is transferable and can enhance a programmer's ability to tackle more complex languages like C and Python in the future.

Definition and Explanation:

Lazarus is an open-source Integrated Development Environment (IDE) used for the Free Pascal Compiler.

It provides a user-friendly platform for software development, primarily focusing on graphical user interfaces (GUIs).

Free Pascal Compiler (FPC): Lazarus uses the FPC, which is a modern Pascal compiler supporting various platforms and architectures.

FPC is known for its compatibility with Delphi, a widely used Pascal-based IDE.

Cross-Platform Development:

One of Lazarus's key features is its ability to create cross-platform applications. Developers can write code once and compile it for different operating systems like Windows, macOS, and Linux.

Component Library:

Lazarus includes a rich component library, called the Lazarus Component Library (LCL), which provides numerous pre-built components for creating GUIs easily and effectively.

***The component information is written in appendix.

Development and Evolution:

Origins:

Lazarus began as a project to provide a free and open-source alternative to Borland's Delphi. Its development started in the late 1990s.

Growth:

Over the years, Lazarus has evolved significantly, adding more features and enhancing compatibility with Delphi, making it an attractive option for Delphi developers looking for a free tool.

Community Support:

The growth of Lazarus has been largely community-driven, with contributions from programmers around the world. This has led to its robust development and wide platform support.

Why Lazarus is Recommended?

Advantages and Benefits:

21

Ease of Use:

Lazarus offers a highly intuitive and user-friendly interface, making it accessible for beginners and students learning programming.

Cross-Platform Development:

Its ability to create cross-platform applications is a significant advantage, allowing developers to target multiple operating systems with a single codebase.

Strong Delphi Compatibility:

For those familiar with Delphi, Lazarus provides a comfortable and free alternative, facilitating a smooth transition.

Rich Component Library:

The extensive component library aids in quick and effective GUI development, reducing the time and effort required for coding standard elements.

Active Community:

The Lazarus community is active and supportive, providing a wealth of resources, documentation, and forums for help and knowledge sharing.

Free and Open-Source:

Being free and open-source, Lazarus is an excellent choice for educational institutions and individuals who prefer a cost-effective development tool.

Regular Updates:

Regular updates and improvements by the community ensure that Lazarus stays current with modern development needs and standards.

What is Lazarus IDE in detail?

Definition:

Lazarus Integrated Development Environment (IDE) is a free, open-source software development platform primarily used for creating graphical and console applications.

It is highly compatible with Delphi, a widely used programming language and environment.

Core Purpose:

Lazarus IDE is designed to streamline the process of developing applications using the Free Pascal compiler.

It facilitates the creation of cross-platform applications with minimal adjustments to the source code.

24

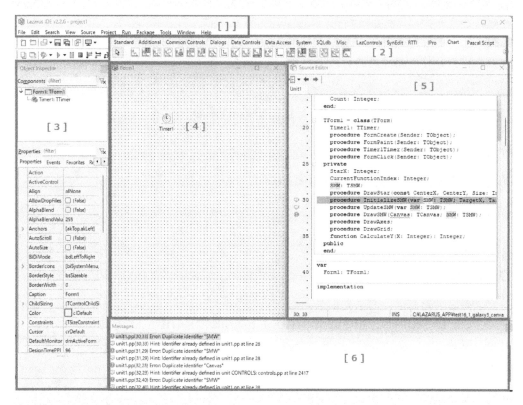

Lazarus IDE Screen Shot

[1] Main Menu

[2] Components

[3] Object Inspector

[4] Form1

[5] Code Editor

[6] Message Window

[1] Main Menu:

Lazarus IDE v2.2.6 - project1

File   Edit   Search   View   Source   Project   Run   Package   Tools   Window   Help

Functionality:

The Main Menu serves as the central hub for accessing various features and functions within the Lazarus IDE. It includes options for file management, editing, project settings, tools, and customization.

User Experience:

Designed for intuitive navigation, the Main Menu organizes all essential functions in a straightforward layout, making it easy for users to find and access the tools and settings they need for their development tasks.

A centralized interface for accessing all key features and tools in Lazarus. For an in-depth exploration of each menu item and its functionalities, refer to the detailed guide in the appendix.

[2] Components:

Functionality:

Components in Lazarus are pre-built elements that can be dragged and dropped onto your application's forms. They include a wide range of controls like buttons, text fields, labels, and more advanced elements like tables and charts.

User Experience:

The component library simplifies the development process by providing a visual way to add functionality to applications. Users can quickly build the interface of their application without writing extensive code, which is particularly beneficial for beginners.

Essential building blocks for creating the user interface and adding functionality to your Lazarus applications. A comprehensive list and description of each component are available in the appendix.

[3] Object Inspector:

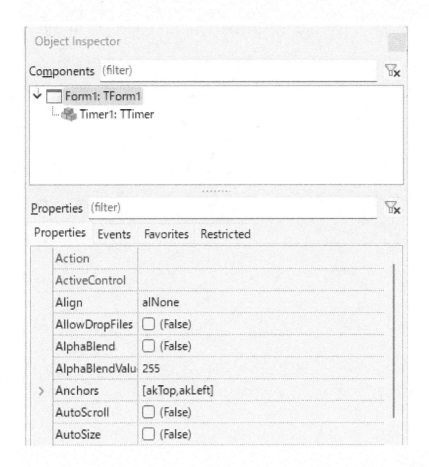

Functionality:

The Object Inspector is a tool used to view and modify the properties and events of selected components in your project. It allows you to customize the appearance and behavior of components at design time.

User Experience:

With its clear and organized interface, the Object Inspector makes it easy to fine-tune the properties of components, enhancing the user's ability to control and customize the application's design and functionality effectively.

A powerful tool for modifying the properties and events of components in your project. Detailed usage instructions and tips for effectively utilizing the Object Inspector can be found in the appendix.

[4] Form1:

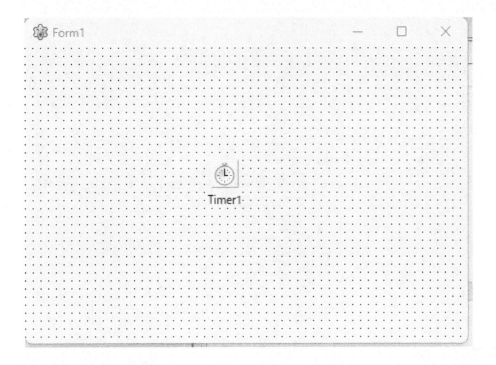

Functionality:

Form1 is the default main form (window) of a new Lazarus application. It serves as the canvas where components are placed and arranged to design the application's user interface.

User Experience:

Form1 provides a straightforward, WYSIWYG (What You See Is What You Get) environment for designing the layout of an application. It allows users to visually construct their application's interface, making the design process more intuitive and interactive.

[5] Code Editor:

```
Source Editor                                              —  □  ×
▸▤ ▾ ⬅ ➡
*Unit1
   .    var
   .        Form1: TForm1;
  125
   .    const
   .  □    // Constants for graphical elements and game mechanics.
   .        StarSize = 20; // Size of the star.
   .        StarColor = clYellow; // Color of the star.
  130        StarLineWidth = 7; // Width of the star's outline.
   .        GraphScale = 100; // Scaling factor for graphing functions.
   .
   .  □    // Array of mathematical functions represented in the game.
   .        GraphFunctions: array[0..4] of Integer = (0, 1, 2, 3, 4);
  135        FunctionTexts: array[0..4] of string = (
   .            'Y = 50 * X^2 - 100', // Quadratic function.
   .            'Y = | 50 * X + 100 |', // Absolute value function.
   .            'Y = 150 * Sin(2 * X)', // Sine function.
   .            'Y = 50 / X (X ≠ 0)', // Inverse function.
  140            'Y = 20 * tan(2.5 * X) (cos(X) ≠ 0)' // Tangent function.
   .        );
   .
```

Functionality:

The core component where you write and edit your Pascal code. It is equipped with features like syntax highlighting, code completion, and error indication.

User Experience:

The editor is tailored to enhance readability and ease the coding process, making it accessible to beginners and efficient for experienced programmers.

The primary workspace for writing and editing Pascal code, featuring syntax highlighting and error indication. For a detailed overview of Pascal grammar and a comprehensive list of error codes, please refer to the appendix.

[6] Message Window:

```
Messages
Compile Project, Target: project1.exe: Success, Hints: 2
  unit1.pp(84,46) Hint: Parameter "Button" not used
  unit1.pp(85,7) Hint: Parameter "Shift" not used
```

Functionality:

The Message Window in Lazarus displays compiler messages, debug information, and other important notifications. It is essential for understanding the compilation process and identifying errors in the code.

User Experience:

This window provides clear and actionable feedback on the code's performance and issues, aiding in the debugging process. Its organized layout helps users quickly locate and resolve problems, streamlining the development workflow.

Conclusion:

In this section, we have explored the fundamental components of the Lazarus Integrated Development Environment (IDE), each playing a crucial role in the development of Pascal applications.

The Main Menu acts as the nerve center, offering access to a wide array of tools and settings essential for project management and development.

The Components provide a rich library of pre-built elements, enabling rapid and visual construction of user interfaces.

The Object Inspector is an invaluable tool for fine-tuning the properties and behaviors of these components, enhancing both the functionality and aesthetics of your application.

Form1 serves as the primary canvas, a starting point where the visual elements of your application come to life.

The Code Editor is where the magic of programming happens, a space where your Pascal code is written, edited, and brought to life, supported by features like syntax highlighting and error indication.

Lastly, the Message Window offers vital feedback during the development process, displaying compiler messages, debug information, and other notifications crucial for troubleshooting and refining your code.

Together, these components form a cohesive and powerful environment in Lazarus, designed to streamline the process of developing robust and efficient Pascal applications.

Whether you are a beginner just starting out in programming or an experienced developer, understanding and utilizing these elements effectively is key to creating successful software projects.

For more detailed information on each component, including Pascal grammar and error codes, be sure to refer to the comprehensive guides provided in the appendix of this book.

1.   Visit the Official Lazarus Website:

•   Open your web browser and go to Lazarus Official Website.

https://www.lazarus-ide.org/

What is Lazarus?

Lazarus is a Delphi compatible cross-platform IDE for Rapid Application Development. It has variety of components ready for use and a graphical form designer to easily create complex graphical user interfaces.

Learn more...   Wikipedia

What can it do?

You can create your own open source or commercial applications. With Lazarus you can create file browsers, image viewers, database applications, graphics editing software, games, 3D software, medical analysis software or any other type of software.

See Application Gallery   Why use it?

Where to learn?

Lazarus has a huge community of people supporting each other. It include scientists and students, pupils and teachers, professionals and hobbyists. Our wiki provides tutorials, documentation and ideas. Our forums and mailing-list offer a space to ask questions and talk to users and the developers.

Start Learning   Books | Online Tutorials

Screenshot of Lazarus official web site as of January,2024

2.   Choose Your Operating System:

•   On the website, you'll find download links for different operating systems. Select the one that matches your system (Windows, macOS, or Linux).

3.   Download the Installer:

***the size of installer for Win is less than 200MB.
But it takes time about 5 minutes.
Please just wait until the finish of downloading.

•   For Windows, you'll typically download an .exe file.

•   For macOS, it's usually a .dmg file.

•   For Linux, the options might include .deb for Debian-based systems, .rpm for Red Hat-based systems, or a tarball for other distributions.

4.   Run the Installer:

•   Windows:

Double-click the downloaded .exe file and follow the installation prompts. You may need administrative privileges.

•   macOS:

Open the .dmg file and drag the Lazarus icon to your Applications folder.

- Linux:

The process varies; for .deb files, you can use sudo dpkg -i filename.deb in the terminal. For .rpm files, use sudo rpm -i filename.rpm. If you downloaded a tarball, extract it and follow any included instructions.

***I checked Lazarus 2.2.6 installation for Windows.
And the installation type is for second version in my Windows11.
I have Lazarus 2.2.2 and Lazarus 2.2.6 at the same time.

For Lazarus beginner those who use Windows11, it is recommended that you should choose Lazarus for Win(64bit) that is latest.

5.   Follow Installation Steps:

- The installer will guide you through the process. Accept the license agreement and choose your preferred settings. Default settings are usually sufficient for beginners.

***default setting = full installation

6.   Wait for Installation to Complete:

- Installation might take a few minutes. Ensure it completes successfully.

7.   Launch Lazarus:

•   After installation, you can launch Lazarus from your applications menu (or equivalent).

•   On the first launch, Lazarus might ask you to configure certain settings. The default options are typically fine for most users.

***You do not have to change the configuration.
Just press OK for everything.

8.   Verify the Installation:

•   Once Lazarus opens, create a new project to test if everything is working correctly. Go to File > New > Project and choose a simple project type, like a Simple Program.

*** For beginner you should select project > application.

*** For beginner I will recommend that you should not change the file name for project1 and unit1 while saving prompt appear. Just press OK button for both to save the files as default name.

•   Write a small test program, for example, a 'Hello, World!' application, and run it to ensure the compiler and IDE are functioning correctly.

*** If you have no knowledge about Lazarus. you already have form1 in your screen.

***To check Lazarus functionality at the first, you don't have to change anything.

***Just select Run>Compile

***Just select Run>Run

***Only the first Compile and Run, you will encounter these messages about technical detail of debug option.

***Enable Dwarf 2 with sets
***Enable Dwarf 2 (-gw)
***Enable Dwarf 3 (-gw3)

***For developing simple 2D game, any button will do.
***I personally select the first one: Enable Dwarf 2 with sets

///

The technical detail for the messages.
You can skip reading these,

Enable Dwarf 2 with sets (-gw):

This option uses the DWARF 2 format with some extensions.
It is a common choice and generally provides good compatibility
and stability for debugging.

Enable Dwarf 2 (-gw):

This is the standard DWARF 2 format without the extensions.
It's another stable option but may lack some features compared
to "Enable Dwarf 2 with sets."

Enable Dwarf 3 (-gw3):

This option uses the newer DWARF 3 format, which includes
more features and improvements over DWARF 2. However, it
might not be as thoroughly tested or widely supported as the
older format.

///

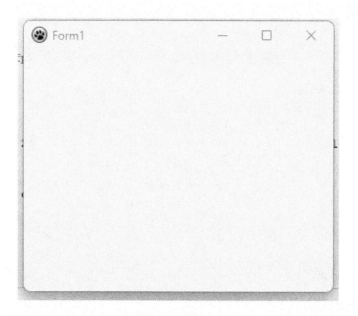

***Then you can see the From1 in the screen. You can check the form can be resize, it can be in task bar by pressing '-' in right upper of the form.

***To terminate the program, you can do below:

***[1] You press x button of form1
***[2] You select Run > Stop
***[3] Press red square mark in the menu.

9.   Update and Configure (Optional):

•   You may want to customize the IDE to suit your preferences. This can be done in the settings or preferences section of the IDE.

***For Japanese Lazarus beginners, I will recommend them to change the language setting to Japanese(ja). For English users, however ,you do not have to change the language setting.

•   Check for updates regularly to keep your Lazarus IDE up-to-date(Optional).

Tips and Considerations:

•   Internet Connection: Make sure you have a stable internet connection during the download and installation process.

•   Administrator Rights: On Windows, you might need administrator rights to install the software.

Finding the Lazarus Executable File in Windows 11

Open File Explorer:

Click on the File Explorer icon on your taskbar or press Windows Key + E to open File Explorer.

Navigate to the Installation Directory:

Go to the directory where you installed Lazarus. If you are not sure where it is, it's commonly found in C:¥Program Files or C:¥Program Files (x86).

Locate Lazarus Folder:

Inside the installation directory, look for a folder named Lazarus or something similar.

Find the Executable:

In the Lazarus folder, look for a file named lazarus. Since Windows 11 might not show file extensions by default, it may appear simply as lazarus with an icon representing an application.

Creating a Shortcut for Lazarus IDE

Right-Click on the Lazarus Executable:

Once you find the lazarus file, right-click on it.

Select 'Create Shortcut':

In the context menu, choose Create shortcut. Windows might prompt that the shortcut will be placed on the desktop instead.

Rename the Shortcut (Optional):

After the shortcut is created, it will appear either in the same folder or on your desktop, named something like lazarus - Shortcut. You can rename it to make it more recognizable. Right-click on the shortcut and select Rename. Then, type Lazarus IDE or any name you prefer and press Enter.

Move the Shortcut to a Desired Location:

If the shortcut is not already on your desktop, you can move it there for easy access. Simply drag the shortcut to your desktop or to any other folder where you want quick access to Lazarus.

Verify the Shortcut:

Double-click on the newly created shortcut to ensure it opens the Lazarus IDE correctly. This step is important to confirm that the shortcut works as intended.

Additional Tips

Change Shortcut Icon (Optional):

If you want to change the icon of the shortcut for better recognition, right-click on the shortcut, select Properties, then click Change Icon. Choose an icon that represents Lazarus IDE for you.

Pin to Taskbar or Start Menu:

For even quicker access, you can pin the Lazarus IDE shortcut to your taskbar or start menu. Right-click on the shortcut and select Pin to Taskbar or Pin to Start.

By following these steps, you can easily locate the Lazarus executable and create a convenient shortcut, ensuring quick and easy access to the Lazarus IDE on your Windows 11 system. This will be helpful for those who do not have the shortcut automatically created during installation.

Steps to Create "Hello World!" in Lazarus with Safe Project Management

Create a New Folder for Your Project:

Before opening Lazarus, create a new folder where you will save your project. This can be done in your file explorer. For example, create a folder named 001_HelloWorld in your Documents or a chosen directory.

Start Lazarus:

Open the Lazarus IDE by clicking on its shortcut.

Create a New Application Project:

In the Lazarus IDE, go to Project in the menu bar.
Select New Project... > Application. A new project will be created with a default form (Form1).

Immediately Save the Project:

Important:

Save your project and unit in the new folder to avoid overwriting other work.

Click File > Save All.

You can keep the default name Project1 and Unit1
In the dialog box, navigate to your 001_HelloWorld folder.

Save **Project1**
Next, save **Unit1**

Design the Form for "Hello World":

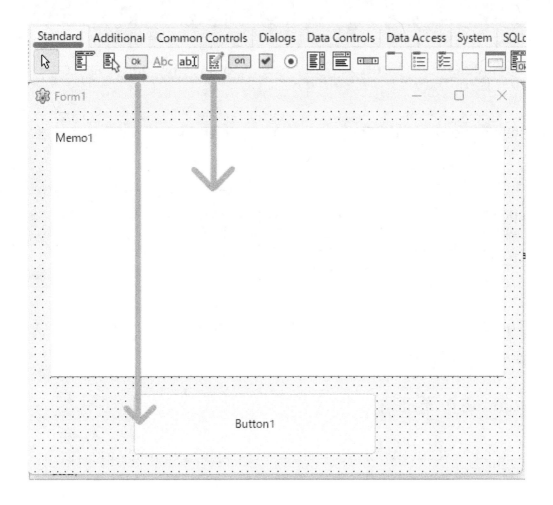

On Form1, add a TMemo and a TButton from the component palette.

Set properties in the Object Inspector.

For example, change the Caption of the TButton to 'Show Message'.(This is optional.)

Add Code to the Button's OnClick Event:

Double-click on the button to open the code editor.

By doubleclicking button1, Lazarus automatically generate code that is for button1 pressing event.

Inside the Button1Click procedure, write the following code:

***You need to input only bold letters like below:

```
procedure TForm1.Button1Click(Sender: TObject);
begin
   Memo1.Lines.Add('Hello World!');
end;
```

This code will output "Hello World!" in the TMemo when the button is clicked.

Run the Program:

You can execute your program using any of the following methods:

[1] Main Menu > Run > Run:

Go to the main menu, select 'Run', and then choose 'Run' from the submenu.

[2] Press F9:

Simply press the F9 key on your keyboard to compile and run the program.

[3] Click the Green Play Icon:

Click on the green play icon in the toolbar to compile and run
your program.

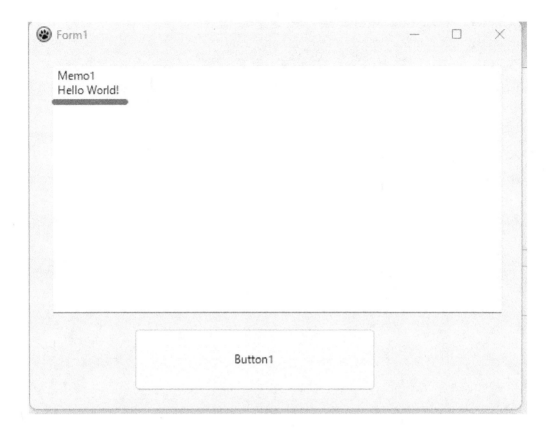

Click the button in the application window to see "Hello World!" appear in the memo.

Regularly Save Your Work:

Make it a habit to regularly save your progress by clicking File > Save All.

By following these steps, you ensure that your "Hello World!" project is safely stored in its own folder, preventing any accidental overwriting of other projects. This practice of organizing and saving work is essential, especially for beginners, to manage multiple projects effectively.

WHAT IS CHATGPT

ChatGPT-4 is a type of advanced computer program known as an AI, or Artificial Intelligence. It's designed to communicate with people in a way that feels natural and human-like. Imagine it as a very smart robot that you can chat with through text.

Here's what makes ChatGPT-4 special:

It Understands and Responds: When you type something to ChatGPT-4, it reads and understands your words, then comes up with a response, much like a human would in a conversation.

It's Really Knowledgeable:

ChatGPT-4 has been trained on a vast amount of information from books, articles, websites, and other sources. This means it can talk about a wide range of topics, from science and history to everyday life questions.

It Learns from Interactions:

While it doesn't learn in real-time from individual users, it has been designed to improve over time based on the data it was trained on. This makes it quite adept at answering questions and providing information.

It's Versatile:

You can use ChatGPT-4 for various purposes, like getting help with homework, generating creative stories, coding assistance, learning new things, or just having an interesting conversation.

It's Respectful of Rules:

ChatGPT-4 is programmed to follow certain guidelines, like not providing harmful or unsafe information, and respecting privacy.

In short, ChatGPT-4 is like a virtual assistant or a chat buddy that's powered by AI, capable of discussing a wide array of topics and assisting with different tasks, all through text-based conversation.

As of January 2024, there are two main versions of ChatGPT available: the free version, which is based on ChatGPT-3.5, and the paid version, which uses ChatGPT-4. Here's a simple explanation of the differences between them:

Version and Capabilities:

ChatGPT-3.5 (Free Version):

This version is based on an earlier model, GPT-3.5. It's quite capable and can handle a wide range of topics, but it may not be as advanced in understanding context or generating responses as the newer version.

ChatGPT-4 (Paid Version):

This is the latest and more advanced version. It has been trained on more data and refined algorithms, which generally means it can provide more accurate, detailed, and context-aware responses.

Performance and Sophistication:

The ChatGPT-4 version is likely to be more sophisticated in its language understanding and generation. It can handle complex queries better and provide more nuanced and coherent responses.

Access to Features:

The paid version may offer exclusive features, such as priority access to new updates, enhanced capabilities, or specialized functionalities that are not available in the free version.

User Experience:

Users of the paid version might experience faster response times and possibly a more refined interaction, as paid services often come with additional support and resources.

In summary, while both versions are powerful tools for conversation and information, ChatGPT-4 offers advancements in performance, sophistication, and exclusive features, reflecting the ongoing development and improvements in AI technology.

Advanced Natural Language Processing:

ChatGPT-4 excels in understanding and generating natural language. This means it can engage in conversations that feel incredibly human-like, making interactions smooth and intuitive.

Customization and Flexibility:

Users can tailor ChatGPT-4 to meet specific needs or preferences. Whether it's for personal use, education, or business, ChatGPT-4 can adapt to various contexts and requirements.

Assistance in Learning and Education:

ChatGPT-4 can be a valuable tool for students and educators. It can assist in explaining complex subjects, provide practice exercises, and even help in learning new languages, making education more interactive and accessible.

Support in Creative Endeavors:

For writers, artists, and creatives, ChatGPT-4 can be a source of inspiration. It can help brainstorm ideas, suggest plot lines, or even co-write stories and scripts, fostering creativity and innovation.

Development of Computer Programs:

ChatGPT-4 can assist in various stages of software development. From conceptualizing algorithms to explaining code snippets in different programming languages, it can be a valuable resource for both novice and experienced programmers.

Enhancing Business Operations:

For businesses, ChatGPT-4 can automate routine tasks, provide customer support through chatbots, and analyze data trends, thereby increasing efficiency and improving customer engagement. It can also assist in drafting business documents, emails, and reports, saving valuable time and resources.

Accessibility and Inclusivity:

ChatGPT-4 can be a tool for making information and services more accessible to a wider audience, including those with disabilities. Its ability to understand and generate text in various languages and formats makes it an inclusive technology.

In essence, ChatGPT-4 is not just a chatbot; it's a versatile AI tool that can enhance various aspects of daily life, work, and creativity. Its advanced capabilities in language processing, combined with its adaptability and wide range of applications, make it a valuable asset in numerous fields, including education, creative arts, software development, and business.

ChatGPT-4: Engaging FAQs with Compelling Examples

Question 1:

How can ChatGPT-4 assist in everyday tasks?

Answer:

ChatGPT-4 can provide personalized assistance for a variety of daily tasks, from cooking to scheduling.

Example:

When asked, "What should I cook tonight?" ChatGPT-4 can suggest a recipe based on the ingredients you have in your kitchen.

Question 2:

In what ways can ChatGPT-4 revolutionize business operations?

Answer:

ChatGPT-4 can offer tailored strategies for marketing, customer service, and data analysis.

Example:

A small business owner receives a custom marketing plan from ChatGPT-4, specifically designed for their target market.

Question 3:

How does ChatGPT-4 contribute to learning and education?

Answer:

ChatGPT-4 can enhance language learning, provide explanations on various subjects, and assist with homework.

Example:

A student practices English conversation with ChatGPT-4 and gets immediate feedback to improve their language skills.

Question 4:

Can ChatGPT-4 fuel creative projects?

Answer:

ChatGPT-4 can inspire creativity by generating ideas for stories, art, and more.

Example:

A writer uses ChatGPT-4 to overcome writer's block by generating unique story ideas and plot lines.

Question 5:

How can ChatGPT-4 support personal health goals?

Answer:

ChatGPT-4 offers advice on wellness, exercise routines, and healthy eating.

Example:

Someone receives daily tips on maintaining a healthy lifestyle, including workout routines and nutritional guidance from hatGPT-4.

Question 6:

What role does ChatGPT-4 play in software development?

Answer:

ChatGPT-4 assists in coding, debugging, and learning new programming languages.

Example:

A beginner coder gets a step-by-step guide from ChatGPT-4 to develop a simple Python application.

Question 7:

How can ChatGPT-4 simplify travel planning?

Answer:

ChatGPT-4 can help plan trips, offering itinerary suggestions and cultural insights.

Example:

ChatGPT-4 helps plan an unforgettable European adventure with a customized itinerary and local tips.

Question 8:

How does ChatGPT-4 enhance hobbies and leisure activities?

Answer:

ChatGPT-4 provides ideas and tips to enrich various hobbies and activities.

Example:

A photography enthusiast gets advice on techniques and local spots for photography from ChatGPT-4.

Question 9:

Can ChatGPT-4 help organize daily schedules and tasks?

Answer:

ChatGPT-4 aids in time management and task prioritization for more efficient daily planning.

Example:

ChatGPT-4 helps a user efficiently plan their weekly schedule, balancing work and personal tasks.

Question 10:

In what ways can ChatGPT-4 aid in personal development?

Answer:

ChatGPT-4 supports goal setting and personal growth with motivational advice and strategies.

Example:

A user receives a personalized guide from ChatGPT-4 for achieving personal goals, along with motivational techniques.

Tips for Effectively Using ChatGPT-4 in Game Development with Lazarus (Pascal)

Point 1: Giving Effective Instructions to ChatGPT-4

Be Specific and Detailed:

Clearly describe what you want to achieve in your game. The more specific you are, the better ChatGPT-4 can assist you.

Break Down Your Requests:

Divide your game development process into smaller, manageable tasks and ask ChatGPT-4 about them one at a time.

Use Step-by-Step Instructions:

When you need code, provide step-by-step instructions on what the code should do. This helps ChatGPT-4 generate more accurate and useful responses.

Provide Context:

Give ChatGPT-4 background information about your game and what you've already done. This helps it understand your project better.

Iterate and Refine:

Use the feedback loop. Start with a basic request, review the response, and then ask follow-up questions to refine the results.

Example Prompt for Creating Code:

"Using Lazarus (Pascal), I want to generate code for a 2D game where the XY coordinate plane is centered on Form1. Can you provide a basic example of how to set up the coordinate system with the origin in the middle of Form1?"

Point 2: Understanding What ChatGPT-4 Can't Do

Code Compilation:

ChatGPT-4 can suggest code, but it can't compile it. Developers need to compile the code in Lazarus (Pascal) to check for syntactical errors. Be aware that the code generated by ChatGPT-4 might contain errors, and developers will need to debug these themselves.

Program Execution:

ChatGPT-4 cannot execute programs. Developers must run their programs in Lazarus and visually check if the output aligns with their expectations. If there are discrepancies, they should provide feedback to ChatGPT-4 for further assistance.

Handling Complex Programs:

As of January 2024, ChatGPT-4 may struggle with understanding complex programs, particularly when the source code exceeds 400-500 lines. This limitation means that developers need to manage and oversee larger codebases themselves.

Partial Optimization in Larger Programs:

In larger programs, ChatGPT-4 tends to provide code optimized for specific parts rather than understanding the entire Unit1. Developers should be aware of this when working on more extensive projects.

These insights are based on a month-long experience of developing a game with ChatGPT-4 and are crucial for users to effectively utilize ChatGPT-4 in their game development endeavors. More detailed individual guidance will be provided in the book

Chapter 3 Overview : Game development

In this chapter, we will delve into the creation of a custom game, written entirely in English. This game is a simple 2D game, conceived and initially developed without the assistance of ChatGPT-4.

The challenge presented here is to explore how much of this game can be further developed in collaboration with ChatGPT-4.

The game, in its essence, is a product of my own ideas, initially crafted from scratch without external aid. The journey of its development, from a mere concept to a playable entity, is a testament to the creative process.

Now, with the integration of ChatGPT-4, we aim to push the boundaries of this development, enhancing and expanding the game's features and functionalities.

In the subsequent chapters, we will cover various aspects of game development in detail:

Chapter 4: Math XY Coordinate - This chapter will focus on the mathematical foundations of the game, particularly the use of XY coordinates in game design. Understanding these concepts is crucial for game mechanics and visual representation.

Chapter 5: Drawing Star Shape with Canvas - Here, we will explore the graphical aspect of the game, specifically how to draw a star shape using only Canvas. This will serve as a fundamental skill for creating other game graphics.

Chapter 6: Star Movement with Math Functions - This chapter will combine the concepts from Chapters 4 and 5, demonstrating how to animate the star shape using mathematical functions to simulate movement.

Chapter 7: Drawing Bullet by Mouse Click - We will learn how to integrate user interactions into the game. This includes drawing and firing bullets in response to mouse clicks, a common feature in many games.

Chapter 8: Hit Judgement - This chapter deals with collision detection, determining when objects in the game, like stars and bullets, interact or collide.

Chapter 9: Score Logic - Here, we will develop the scoring system of the game, an essential element for engaging and motivating players. We'll discuss how to track and update scores based on game events, such as hitting targets or achieving certain milestones.

Chapter 10: Game Over Logic - In this chapter, we will develop what is the score, how to accept space key to reply. This is typical game end style especially for retro game. By pressing space key game is reset and new game will start.

Chapter 11: Full Unit 1 Program Code - The final chapter will present the complete code for Unit 1 of the game. This will serve as a comprehensive guide and reference for the game's development up to this point, showcasing the integration of all the concepts and techniques discussed in the previous chapters.

Chapter 12 further development for your enjoyment – In this chapter, you will see three suggestions. Easy level, adjustment only change const values. Middle level, changing some value in the code. Advanced level, adding 3 math graphs in this game.

Throughout these chapters, the focus will be on practical application and hands-on development. By the end of this section, readers should have a clear understanding of the basic principles of game development and how to apply them using modern tools and technologies, with a special emphasis on the role and capabilities of ChatGPT-4 in this creative process.

Material for Math Teacher

This book, while primarily focused on game development, offers a unique opportunity for mathematics teachers to enhance their teaching methods.

By utilizing the content of this book, teachers can demonstrate mathematical functions through the movement of stars in a game environment, making it easier for students to grasp the concept of functions.

As the game progresses, function names and the coordinates of the stars will be displayed in real-time, moving along the XY coordinate plane. This visual representation aids in explaining abstract mathematical concepts in a more tangible and engaging way.

For those who are keen on game creation, I encourage a thorough reading of the entire book.

The journey from basic concepts to advanced game development techniques is both informative and inspiring.

Additionally, this book includes a comprehensive appendix, which provides detailed explanations of PASCAL syntax and Lazarus, a powerful tool for game development.

These resources are designed to be user-friendly for both instructors and learners, making this book a valuable asset for anyone interested in the field of game development and programming.

In summary, whether you are a mathematics teacher looking to bring a new dimension to your classroom, or an aspiring game developer eager to learn the ropes of game programming, this book offers a wealth of knowledge and practical applications that cater to both educational and creative pursuits.

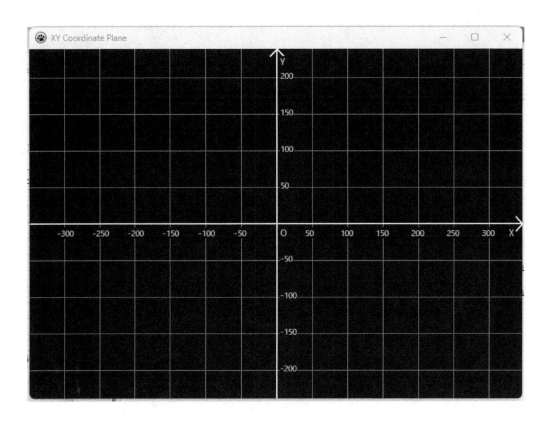

In this chapter, I am going to tell you how to draw XY Coordinate by Lazarus(Pascal).This program can be used to those who use this program for mathematical purpose or game development purposes. I am going to show all source code and give you in detail explanation for that.

This Lazarus Pascal program is a simple yet effective demonstration of creating an XY coordinate plane within a

70

graphical user interface. Designed for complete beginners, it showcases fundamental concepts such as form creation, custom drawing, and basic geometry.

The program is structured around a single form, TForm1, which serves as the canvas for drawing. The **FormCreate procedure** initializes the form with a title, and the **FormPaint procedure** is where the actual drawing occurs. This is triggered whenever the form needs to be redrawn, such as when it's first displayed or resized.

Key to this program are three custom procedures: **DrawAxes**, **DrawGrid**, and **DrawAxisNumbers**.

DrawAxes draws the X and Y axes, complete with arrowheads and labels ('X', 'Y', and 'O' for the origin). This helps in understanding the orientation of the coordinate system. The axes are drawn in white for clear visibility against the black background set in **FormPaint**.

DrawGrid creates a grid on the form, with lines spaced 50 units apart. This grid aids in visualizing distances and positions on the plane. The grid lines are drawn in gray, providing a subtle yet useful reference.

Finally, **DrawAxisNumbers** adds numerical labels to the axes at every 50 units, enhancing the grid's utility for mathematical purposes. These labels help in identifying specific points and distances on the plane.

Overall, this program is an excellent starting point for beginners to explore graphical programming in Lazarus(Pascal) and understand basic coordinate geometry. It's a practical example of how programming can be used to visualize and interact with mathematical concepts.

```
unit Unit1;

{$mode objfpc}{$H+}

interface

uses
  Classes, SysUtils, Forms, Controls, Graphics, ExtCtrls, Math;

type
  TForm1 = class(TForm)
    procedure FormCreate(Sender: TObject);
    procedure FormPaint(Sender: TObject);
  private
    procedure DrawAxes;
    procedure DrawGrid;
    procedure DrawAxisNumbers;
  public
  end;

var
  Form1: TForm1;

implementation

{$R *.lfm}

{ TForm1 }

// Initializes the form.
procedure TForm1.FormCreate(Sender: TObject);
begin
  Caption := 'XY Coordinate Plane';
end;
```

```
// Handles the painting of the form.
procedure TForm1.FormPaint(Sender: TObject);
begin
   Canvas.Brush.Color := clBlack; // Set background color to
black
   Canvas.FillRect(ClientRect);    // Fill the form with the
background color
   DrawGrid;                        // Draw the grid
   DrawAxes;                        // Draw the axes
   DrawAxisNumbers;                  // Draw numbers on the
axes
end;

// Draws the X and Y axes with labels and arrows.
procedure TForm1.DrawAxes;
const
   ArrowSize = 10; // Size of the arrows at the end of the axes
begin
   Canvas.Pen.Color := clWhite; // Set pen color to white for
axes
   Canvas.Pen.Width := 2;        // Set pen width for axes
   Canvas.Font.Color := clWhite; // Set font color to white for
labels

   // Draw X-axis
   Canvas.MoveTo(0, ClientHeight div 2);
   Canvas.LineTo(ClientWidth, ClientHeight div 2);
   // Arrow for X-axis
   Canvas.LineTo(ClientWidth - ArrowSize, (ClientHeight div 2) -
ArrowSize);
   Canvas.MoveTo(ClientWidth, ClientHeight div 2);
   Canvas.LineTo(ClientWidth - ArrowSize, (ClientHeight div 2)
+ ArrowSize);

   // Draw Y-axis
   Canvas.MoveTo(ClientWidth div 2, ClientHeight);
   Canvas.LineTo(ClientWidth div 2, 0);
   // Arrow for Y-axis
   Canvas.LineTo((ClientWidth div 2) - ArrowSize, ArrowSize);
   Canvas.MoveTo(ClientWidth div 2, 0);
   Canvas.LineTo((ClientWidth div 2) + ArrowSize, ArrowSize);

   // Labels for axes
   Canvas.TextOut(ClientWidth - 20, ClientHeight div 2 + 5,
'X');
   Canvas.TextOut(ClientWidth div 2 + 5, 10, 'Y'); // Adjusted
position for 'Y' label
```

```
    Canvas.TextOut(ClientWidth div 2 + 5, ClientHeight div 2 +
5, 'O');
end;

// Draws the grid on the form.
procedure TForm1.DrawGrid;
var
  i: Integer;
  GridSpacing: Integer = 50; // Spacing for the grid lines
begin
  Canvas.Pen.Color := clGray; // Set pen color for grid lines
  Canvas.Pen.Width := 1;      // Set pen width for grid lines

  // Draw grid lines
  for i := -ClientWidth div 2 to ClientWidth div 2 do
  begin
    if (i mod GridSpacing = 0) and (i <> 0) then
    begin
      Canvas.MoveTo(i + (ClientWidth div 2), 0);
      Canvas.LineTo(i + (ClientWidth div 2), ClientHeight);
      Canvas.MoveTo(0, i + (ClientHeight div 2));
      Canvas.LineTo(ClientWidth, i + (ClientHeight div 2));
    end;
  end;
end;

// Draws numbers on the axes at every 50 units.
procedure TForm1.DrawAxisNumbers;
var
  i: Integer;
  GridSpacing: Integer = 50; // Spacing for the numbers on
the grid lines
begin
  Canvas.Font.Color := clWhite; // Set font color to white for
numbers

  // Draw numbers along X-axis
  for i := -ClientWidth div 2 to ClientWidth div 2 do
  begin
    if (i mod GridSpacing = 0) and (i <> 0) then
    begin
      Canvas.TextOut(i + (ClientWidth div 2) - 10,
(ClientHeight div 2) + 5, IntToStr(i));
    end;
  end;

  // Draw numbers along Y-axis
  for i := -ClientHeight div 2 to ClientHeight div 2 do
```

```
  begin
    if (i mod GridSpacing = 0) and (i <> 0) then
    begin
      Canvas.TextOut((ClientWidth div 2) + 5, i +
(ClientHeight div 2) - 10, IntToStr(-i));
    end;
  end;
end;

end.
```

Let's break down the program step-by-step:

Unit Declaration:

The program starts with unit Unit1;. In Lazarus (a Pascal IDE), a unit is like a chapter in a book. It contains code that can be used by other parts of the program or even by other programs. Unit1 is the default name for the first unit in a new project.

Interface Section:

The interface section declares which parts of this unit are available to other units. This includes used units like Classes, SysUtils, Forms, etc., which are libraries of pre-written code that provide useful functions and procedures.

Type Declaration:

Inside the type section, TForm1 = class(TForm) declares a new class TForm1 as a type of TForm. TForm is a basic form or window, and TForm1 is our customized version of it.

Form Procedures:

Procedures like FormCreate and FormPaint are declared. These are specific actions (methods) that TForm1 can perform. FormCreate is called when the form is first created, and FormPaint is called whenever the form needs to be redrawn.

Private Section:

This section contains declarations of procedures that are used internally by the form. In this program, DrawAxes, DrawGrid, and DrawAxisNumbers are such procedures, each responsible for drawing different parts of the coordinate plane.

Global Variable:

var Form1: TForm1;

declares a global variable Form1 of the type TForm1. This is the actual form that will appear when the program runs.

Implementation Section: The implementation section contains the actual code for the procedures declared above. $R *.lfm links this unit to a form file that defines the layout of the form.

FormCreate Procedure:

In FormCreate, properties of the form are set, like its caption (title).

FormPaint Procedure:

FormPaint is where the drawing happens. It sets the background color and calls DrawGrid, DrawAxes, and DrawAxisNumbers to draw the coordinate plane.

Drawing Procedures:

DrawAxes draws the X and Y axes, DrawGrid creates a grid background, and DrawAxisNumbers adds numerical labels to the axes.

Creating Event Handlers Manually in Lazarus:

When you're not using code generated by ChatGPT, you typically create event handlers (like OnCreate for a form) manually.

In Lazarus, this is done using the Object Inspector. Select your form (Form1) in the Object Inspector, then click on the "Events" tab.

Find the OnCreate event. Next to it, there's a button with "..." – clicking this creates a template procedure for the OnCreate event in your code editor. This is where you can add your custom code that should run when the form is created.

Using Code Generated by ChatGPT:

If ChatGPT provides you with a complete unit of code (like Unit1), it might already include procedures for events like OnCreate.

After copying and pasting this code into your Lazarus code editor, you still need to link these procedures to the actual events in the Object Inspector. This step is crucial.

Go to the Object Inspector, find the OnCreate event under the "Events" tab for Form1, and click the "..." button. Lazarus will either take you to the existing OnCreate procedure in the code, or you might need to select it from a list. This step ensures that your OnCreate procedure is correctly connected to the Form1 creation event.

Important Note for Beginners:

Even if you copy and paste the complete code into Lazarus, if you don't link the event handlers (like OnCreate) in the Object Inspector, they won't be executed. Your program might compile without errors, but the OnCreate code won't run, leading to unexpected behavior.

This linking step in the Object Inspector is essential to ensure that your event-handling code is executed at the right time (e.g., when the form is created for OnCreate). I am going to discuss this matter in detail with screenshot.

If you have problem, please follow these steps.

[1] Create New project in Lazarus for XY Coordinate.
[2] Copy and Paste the code into Lazarus Code editor.
    Or you can write the code by your typing.
[3] Setting Object inspector.
[4] Compile the program
[5] Run the program.

I am going to tell you **the step3 Setting Object inspector** in detail.

This setting is very important when you develop programs by Lazarus with ChatGPT.

When using the provided Lazarus program to draw an XY coordinate plane, it's important to correctly set up the event handlers in the Object Inspector after copying the code. Here's a step-by-step guide in English on how to do this:

Setting Up Event Handlers in Lazarus

Understanding the Interface Section:

In the provided code, focus on the interface section, specifically where TForm1 is defined:

```
TForm1 = class(TForm)
    procedure FormCreate(Sender: TObject);
    procedure FormPaint(Sender: TObject);
```

These lines declare two procedures, FormCreate and FormPaint, which are event handlers for the Form1.

Configuring FormCreate:

After copying the code into Lazarus, you need to link the FormCreate event to the actual form.

First, select Form1 in the Object Inspector.
Then, click on the "Events" tab located in the middle of the Object Inspector.

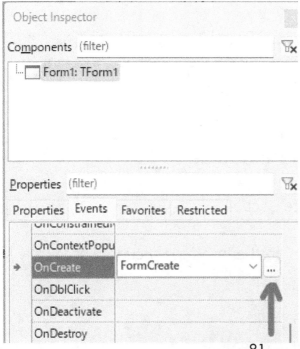

Find OnCreate in the list of events.
Click the "..." button at the right end of the OnCreate event. This action will link the FormCreate procedure in your code to the OnCreate event of Form1.

Configuring FormPaint:

Similarly, for the FormPaint event handler, select Form1 in the Object Inspector.

Again, click on the "Events" tab.

Find OnPaint in the list of events.
Click the "..." button at the right end of the OnPaint event. This will link the FormPaint procedure in your code to the OnPaint event of Form1.

Important Note

Be aware that the names in the Object Inspector might slightly differ from those in the code. It's crucial to correctly identify and link the corresponding events (OnCreate and OnPaint) to the procedures (FormCreate and FormPaint) you have in your code.

By following these steps, you ensure that the event handlers FormCreate and FormPaint are correctly set up in Lazarus, allowing the XY coordinate plane to be drawn as intended when the program runs. This setup is essential for the program to function correctly.

**If you have unknown error message, when you click on the "..." button. I will recommend that you should create new project. In that case something wrong. And this will save your time rather than debugging what is wrong in whole project.

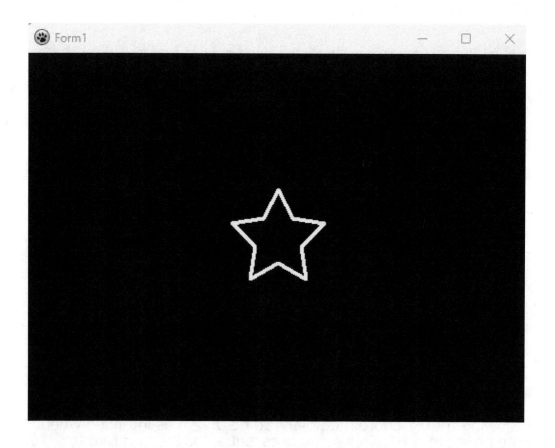

In this chapter, I am going to tell you how to draw star in Lazarus. The start is used in my game and that is drawn canvas.

Let's get started.

Procedure to Draw a Five-Pointed Star

Defining Constants:

StarSize:

This constant defines the size of the star. It determines how far each point of the star extends from the center.

NumPoints:

This represents the number of points in the star, which is 5 for a standard star shape.

Initializing Variables:

An array Points of TPoint is declared to store the coordinates of each point of the star. Since a five-pointed star has 10 distinct points (including inner points), the array size is set to 10.

Calculating Star Points:

The procedure uses a for loop to calculate the coordinates of each point of the star.
For each point, two coordinates are calculated: one for the tip of the star and one for the inner vertex between the tips.
The Angle variable is used to determine the position of each point. It is calculated using the formula -Pi / 2 + (i * 2 * Pi / NumPoints), where i is the current iteration of the loop.
The X and Y coordinates for each point are calculated using trigonometric functions (Cos and Sin) based on the angle and StarSize. These coordinates are adjusted to place the star at the center of the form (ClientWidth / 2 and ClientHeight / 2).

Drawing the Star:

The Canvas.Pen.Color and Canvas.Pen.Width properties are set to define the color and line width of the star's outline.

Canvas.Brush.Style is set to bsClear to make the inside of the star transparent.
Finally, Canvas.Polygon(Points) is called to draw the star. This function connects all the points in the Points array, creating the star shape.

This procedure effectively creates a visually appealing five-pointed star at the center of the form, demonstrating the use of geometry, trigonometry, and graphics programming in Lazarus.

```
unit Unit1;

{$mode objfpc}{$H+}

interface

uses
  Classes, SysUtils, Forms, Controls, Graphics;

type
  // TForm1 is the main form class for the application.
  TForm1 = class(TForm)
    procedure FormPaint(Sender: TObject); // Called for
drawing on the form.
  private
    // Procedure to draw a star at the center of the form.
    procedure DrawStar;
  public
  end;

var
  Form1: TForm1;

implementation

{$R *.lfm}

{ TForm1 }

// This procedure is called when the form needs repainting.
procedure TForm1.FormPaint(Sender: TObject);
begin
  DrawStar; // Draw the star at the center of the form.
end;

// Draws a five-pointed star at the center of the form.
procedure TForm1.DrawStar;
const
  StarSize = 50; // Size of the star.
  NumPoints = 5; // Number of points in the star. Thia value
should be 5.
```

```
var
   Points: array[0..9] of TPoint; // Array to store the points of
the star.
   i: Integer;
   Angle: Double;
begin
   // Calculate the points of the star.
   for i := 0 to NumPoints - 1 do
   begin
      Angle := -Pi / 2 + (i * 2 * Pi / NumPoints);
      Points[i * 2].X := Round(ClientWidth / 2 + StarSize *
Cos(Angle));
      Points[i * 2].Y := Round(ClientHeight / 2 + StarSize *
Sin(Angle));

      Angle := -Pi / 2 + ((i + 0.5) * 2 * Pi / NumPoints);
      Points[i * 2 + 1].X := Round(ClientWidth / 2 + StarSize *
Cos(Angle) / 2);
      Points[i * 2 + 1].Y := Round(ClientHeight / 2 + StarSize *
Sin(Angle) / 2);
   end;

   // Draw the star by connecting the points.
   form1.color := clblack;
   Canvas.Pen.Color := clyellow; // Set the color of the star.
   Canvas.Pen.Width := 4;       // Set the width of the star's
lines.
   Canvas.Brush.Style := bsClear; // Set the brush style.

   Canvas.Polygon(Points); // Draw the star.
end;

end.
```

What need to be done

[1] Creae new project for start object
[2] Copy and Paste the source code to your editor
[3] Object inspector setting
[4] Compile the program
[5] Run the program

I am going to tell you how to set up your object inspector.

```
uses
   Classes, SysUtils, Forms, Controls, Graphics;

type
   // TForm1 is the main form class for the application.
   TForm1 = class(TForm)
      procedure FormPaint(Sender: TObject); // Called for
drawing on the form.
   private
      // Procedure to draw a star at the center of the form.
      procedure DrawStar;
   public
   end;
```

In this program, you will find Procedure FormPaint() under
TForm1 = class(TForm).
This setting must be done by object inspector.

Whatever program made by ChatGPT, you always care about the
procedures under TForm1 = class(TForm) for objector setting.

Setting Up Event Handlers in Lazarus

Open the Object Inspector:

After copying the source code into Lazarus, open the Object
Inspector. This tool is used to set properties and event handlers
for components in your application.

Select Form1:

In the Object Inspector, make sure Form1 is selected. This is the form on which the star will be drawn.

Setting up the OnPaint Event:

Click on the "Events" tab in the Object Inspector. This tab lists all the events that can be handled for the selected component.

Find the OnPaint event in the list. This event is triggered whenever the form needs to be redrawn, which includes the initial drawing of the form.

Click the "..." button next to the OnPaint event. Lazarus will either automatically link this event to the FormPaint procedure in your code, or it will open a dialog where you can select FormPaint from a list of available procedures.

Important Note

Correct Linking: It's crucial to ensure that the OnPaint event is correctly linked to the FormPaint procedure. Without this linkage, the code to draw the star will not execute when the form is redrawn.

By following these steps, you link the drawing logic in your code to the actual rendering process of the form. This setup is essential for the star to be drawn correctly on Form1 when the program runs.

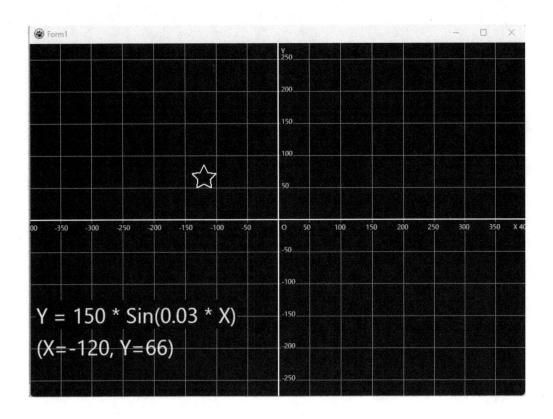

In This Chapter, I am going to tell you how to draw moving start by Mathematical functions.

This program can be used to educational purpose, either for teacher or students. Please feel free to use this program without my permission.

First, We need form1 and Timer1.

You can find Timer1 component from System Tab.
When you do mouse over of the component you will see the text.
Timer1 is very important component for Lazarus programing.
And timer1 is not shown when you execute the program.

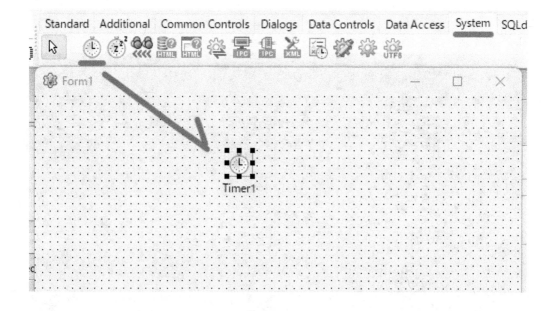

Understanding Coordinate Systems:

Mathematical vs. Lazarus's Form1

Lazarus From1   Mathematics

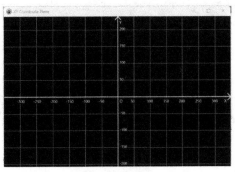

O : Left Top   O : Center
X : Right   X : Right
Y : Down   Y : Up

When developing 2D games in Lazarus, it's crucial to understand the differences between the traditional mathematical XY coordinate plane and the coordinate system used in Lazarus's Form1. Let's explore these differences to provide a clear understanding for beginners.

Traditional Mathematical XY Coordinate Plane

In standard mathematics, the coordinate plane is a two-dimensional plane formed by the intersection of two perpendicular lines called axes, labeled the X and Y axes.

Origin:

The point where these axes intersect is called the origin, typically located at the center of the plane.

X-Axis:

Extends horizontally, with positive values to the right of the origin and negative values to the left.

Y-Axis:

Extends vertically, with positive values above the origin and negative values below.

This system is fundamental in mathematics and forms the basis for plotting points, lines, and shapes in a two-dimensional space.

Lazarus's Form1 Coordinate System

Lazarus, a popular tool for developing applications and games, uses a different approach for its coordinate system in Form1.

Origin:

In Lazarus's Form1, the origin (0,0) is located at the top-left corner of the form, not at the center.

X-Axis:

Similar to traditional mathematics, the X-axis extends horizontally. However, in Lazarus, all X values are positive as you move right from the origin.

Y-Axis:

Contrary to the mathematical Y-axis, in Lazarus, the Y-axis extends downwards from the origin, with all Y values being positive as you move down.

This adjustment in the coordinate system is tailored for computer graphics where the top-left corner is often the starting point for rendering elements on the screen.

Comparing the Two Systems

Understanding these differences is key for beginners transitioning from mathematical concepts to computer graphics in Lazarus:

Origin Location:

Center of the plane (Mathematics) vs. Top-left corner of Form1 (Lazarus).

Y-Axis Direction:

Upwards (Mathematics) vs. Downwards (Lazarus).

By grasping these distinctions, beginners can effectively plot and animate objects in Lazarus, adapting their mathematical knowledge to the specifics of computer graphics.

In our Lazarus project, we're going to use some mathematical functions to animate a star on the screen. These functions are not just mathematical formulas; they have been carefully adjusted to make the animation more engaging and fun.

Setting Up Functions and Their Display Texts
First, we prepare an array of functions and their corresponding display texts. These texts will be shown on the screen, helping users understand what mathematical formula is currently animating the star.

```
GraphFunctions: array[0..4] of Integer = (0, 1, 2, 3, 4);
FunctionTexts: array[0..4] of string = (
   'Y = 0.0077 * X^2 - 150',
   'Y = |0.5 * X + 100|',
   'Y = 150 * Sin(0.03 * X)',
   'Y = 7000 / X (X ≠ 0)',
   'Y = 20 * tan(0.0099 * X) (cos(0.0099X) ≠ 0)'
);
```

Each function has a unique effect on how the star moves on the screen.

Calculating Y-Coordinate in the Program

The CalculateY function is where the magic happens. It takes an X-coordinate as input and calculates the corresponding Y-coordinate based on the selected mathematical function.

```
function TForm1.CalculateY(X: Integer): Integer;

  // ... [Code omitted for simplicity] ...

case GraphFunctions[CurrentFunctionIndex] of
    0: Result := Round(0.0077 * Power(X, 2)-150);
    1: Result := Round(Abs(0.5 * X +100 ));
    2: Result := Round(150 * Sin(0.03 * X));
    3: if X <> 0 then

        Result := Round(9000 / X)
      else
        Result := 0;
    4: if Cos(0.0099 * X) <> 0 then
        Result := Round(10*Sin(0.0099 * X) / Cos(0.0099 *
X))
      else
        Result := 0;
  else
    Result := 0;
  end;

  Result := - Result; // From1's Y direction is downward
end;
```

Here's a breakdown of what happens inside this function:

Case Statement:

Depending on the current function selected, a different
mathematical formula is applied to calculate Y.

Handling Special Cases:

We've included checks to avoid the famous 'Division By Zero' error. For example, when X is 0 in certain functions, we handle it to avoid this error.

Inverting Y-Coordinate:

Since in Lazarus's Form1, the Y-axis extends downwards, we invert the result to align with this coordinate system.

Examples of Function Calculations

Parabolic Motion:

$Y = 0.0077 * X^2 - 150$ creates a parabolic trajectory.

Absolute Linear Function:

$Y = |0.5 * X + 100|$ gives a V-shaped path.

Sinusoidal Path:

$Y = 150 * Sin(0.03 * X)$ creates wave-like motion.

Hyperbolic Path:

$Y = 7000 / X$ (adjusted to avoid division by zero) gives a hyperbolic trajectory.

Tangential Motion:

$Y = 20 * tan(0.0099 * X)$ (with cosine check to avoid division by zero) creates a tangential path.

Each of these functions will make the star move in a unique and interesting way, making the program visually appealing and fun to interact with.

Lazarus Functions Used in the Code

Round()

Purpose:

This function rounds a floating-point number to the nearest integer.

Usage in Code:

It is used to ensure that the result of the mathematical calculations is an integer, as the Result variable is of type Integer.

Example: Round(2.5) will return 3.

Abs()

Purpose:

The Abs function returns the absolute value of a number.

Usage in Code:

It is used to ensure that the result is always positive, regardless of whether the input value is positive or negative.

Example: Abs(-5) will return 5.

Power()

Purpose:

This function raises a number to a specified power.
Usage in Code: It is used to calculate the square of X in the first mathematical function.

Example:

Power(3, 2) will return 9 (since 3 squared is 9).

Sin()

Purpose:

The Sin function calculates the sine of an angle (in radians).

Usage in Code:

It is used to create a sinusoidal path for the star's movement.

Example: Sin(Pi/2) will return 1 (sine of 90 degrees).

Cos()

Purpose:

Similar to Sin, the Cos function calculates the cosine of an angle (in radians).

Usage in Code:

It is used in the last function to check if the cosine of the given value is not zero (to avoid division by zero) and in the calculation of the tangential motion.

Example:

Cos(Pi) will return -1 (cosine of 180 degrees).

Additional Note

The Result := -Result; line at the end of the function inverts the Y-coordinate. This is necessary because in Lazarus's Form1, the Y-axis extends downwards, which is opposite to the traditional mathematical coordinate system where the Y-axis extends upwards.

Continuous Increment of X-Coordinate

Initial Value:

The star's initial X-coordinate (StarX) is set to the left of the form's center. This is the starting point of the star's horizontal movement.

Increment in Timer1Timer:

In each cycle of the timer (triggered by Timer1.Interval), StarX is incremented by a fixed value (StarMoveStep). This consistent incrementation creates a smooth horizontal movement across the form.

Calculation of Y-Coordinate Based on Mathematical Functions
Function Selection:

The Y-coordinate of the star is determined by a mathematical function. The function used at any given time is indicated by CurrentFunctionIndex.

CalculateY Method:

This function is the core of the Y-coordinate calculation. It takes the current StarX value and applies the selected mathematical function to calculate StarY.

The CalculateY Function: A Closer Look

Case Structure:

101

Based on CurrentFunctionIndex, a different mathematical formula is applied:

Parabolic Motion:

For index 0, a quadratic function is used ($Y = 0.0077 * X^2 - 150$).

Linear and Absolute Value:

For index 1, a linear function with an absolute value is used ($Y = |0.5 * X + 100|$).

Sinusoidal Motion:

For index 2, a sine function is used ($Y = 150 * Sin(0.03 * X)$).

Hyperbolic Motion:

For index 3, a reciprocal function is used ($Y = 9000 / X$), with a check to avoid division by zero.

Tangential Motion:

For index 4, a tangent function is used ($Y = 10 * Sin(0.0099 * X) / Cos(0.0099 * X)$), again with a check to avoid division by zero.

Result Inversion:

After calculation, Result is inverted (Result := -Result). This is crucial because the Y-axis in Lazarus's Form1 extends downwards, opposite to the traditional mathematical coordinate system.

Animation Loop: Timer1Timer

Horizontal Movement: Each time the timer triggers, StarX is increased, moving the star horizontally.

Function Switching:

Once StarX exceeds the form's width, it resets, and CurrentFunctionIndex changes, selecting a new mathematical function for the next cycle.

Redrawing:

The form is redrawn (Invalidate), which triggers FormPaint. Here, StarY is recalculated with the updated StarX, and the star is redrawn at its new position.

Result:

Dynamic Y-Coordinate Calculation
The star's Y-coordinate dynamically changes as StarX increases. This change is governed by the mathematical function currently in use.

The continuous horizontal movement combined with the dynamically calculated vertical position creates an animation where the star follows the path of the mathematical function.

Traditional Mathematical XY Coordinate Plane vs. Form1's
Coordinate System

Mathematical Plane:

In standard mathematics, the origin (0,0) is typically at the
center of the plane, with the Y-axis extending upwards.

Form1's System:

In Lazarus's Form1, the origin is at the top-left corner, and the
Y-axis extends downwards.
How the Program Resolves These Differences

Adjusting the Origin:

Initial Positioning: The star's initial X-coordinate (StarX) is set
relative to the center of Form1, not the top-left corner. This is
achieved by starting StarX at a negative value, effectively moving
it to the left of the center.

Horizontal Movement:

As StarX increases, the star moves rightward from this central
starting point, simulating a movement from the left to the right
of a traditional mathematical origin.

Inverting the Y-Axis:

Calculation in CalculateY:

The Y-coordinate (StarY) is calculated using the selected mathematical function. However, since Form1's Y-axis extends downwards, the result of this calculation would be inverted relative to a traditional mathematical plane.

Inversion Adjustment:

To correct this, the result from CalculateY is inverted (Result := -Result). This inversion aligns the calculated Y-coordinate with the traditional mathematical plane's upward Y-axis direction.
Final Positioning of the Star:

Vertical Adjustment:

After calculating StarY, an additional adjustment is made:

StarY := CalculateY(StarX) + (ClientHeight div 2). This

adjustment moves the star vertically to a position that is symmetrical to the center of Form1's height, aligning it with where the horizontal axis would be in a traditional mathematical plane.

Horizontal Adjustment:

When drawing the star in FormPaint, StarX is adjusted to the center of the form's width: StarX + (ClientWidth div 2). This centers the star's horizontal movement around the form's vertical axis, akin to moving across the traditional mathematical X-axis.

For example , if the Form1 size is 800x600,

ClientWidth div 2 = 800 / 2 = 400

ClientHeight div 2 = 600 / 2 = 300

And the point (400, 300) means center of the Form1

Result:

Alignment with Traditional Mathematical Plane
These adjustments in the program ensure that the star's movement on Form1 mimics how it would appear on a traditional mathematical XY coordinate plane.

The star starts its movement from the left of the central vertical axis (like starting from the left of the origin in a mathematical plane) and moves rightward.
The Y-coordinate calculations are inverted to reflect the upward direction of the traditional Y-axis, despite Form1's downward-extending Y-axis.

Displaying the Function Name: DrawFunctionText

Purpose:

This procedure displays the name of the current mathematical function being used to calculate the star's Y-coordinate.

Implementation:

The function name is retrieved from the FunctionTexts array using CurrentFunctionIndex.

The text is displayed at a fixed position on the form (FunctionTextPositionX, FunctionTextPositionY), ensuring it's always visible and not obscured by the moving star.

The font color (FunctionTextFontColor) and size (FunctionTextFontSize) are set to enhance readability against the form's background.

Displaying Star Coordinates: DrawStarCoordinates

Purpose:

This procedure shows the real-time coordinates of the star as it moves across the screen.

Implementation:

The coordinates are formatted into a string representation, typically in the format (X=..., Y=...).

The Y-coordinate displayed is adjusted to reflect the traditional mathematical plane. Since the Y-coordinate is inverted in the calculation (to align with the upward Y-axis of a mathematical plane), it's re-inverted here for display: Y := -Y + (ClientHeight div 2).

The coordinates are displayed at a fixed position on the form (StarCoordPositionX, StarCoordPositionY), similar to the function name, ensuring they are always visible and not overlapping with the star.

Integration with Star Movement

Both the function name and the star's coordinates are updated in real-time as part of the FormPaint procedure. This ensures that they are refreshed every time the form is redrawn, which happens every time the timer triggers and the star's position is updated.

This real-time update provides an interactive and educational experience, allowing viewers to see not only how the star moves according to the mathematical function but also to understand the exact function being used and the star's current position at any given moment.

In summary, the display of the function name and the star's coordinates in your program serves as an informative overlay that complements the visual animation of the star. It provides an educational insight into the underlying mathematics driving the star's movement, enhancing the overall understanding of the program's functionality.

```
unit Unit1;

{$mode objfpc}{$H+}

interface

uses
  Classes, SysUtils, Forms, Controls, Graphics, ExtCtrls, Math;

type
  TForm1 = class(TForm)
    Timer1: TTimer;
    procedure FormCreate(Sender: TObject);
    procedure FormPaint(Sender: TObject);
    procedure Timer1Timer(Sender: TObject);
  private
    StarX: Integer;
    CurrentFunctionIndex: Integer;
    procedure DrawStar(const CenterX, CenterY, Size: Integer;
                       const LineColor: TColor; const
LineWidth: Integer);
    procedure DrawAxes;
    procedure DrawGrid;
    procedure DrawFunctionText;
    procedure DrawStarCoordinates(X, Y: Integer);
    function CalculateY(X: Integer): Integer;
  public
  end;

var
  Form1: TForm1;

const
  StarSize = 20;
  StarColor = clYellow;
  StarLineWidth = 2;
  GraphScale = 50;
```

```
  GraphFunctions: array[0..4] of Integer = (0, 1, 2, 3, 4);
  FunctionTexts: array[0..4] of string = (
    'Y = 0.0077 * X^2 - 150',
    'Y = |0.5 * X + 100|',
    'Y = 150 * Sin(0.03 * X)',
    'Y = 7000 / X (X ≠ 0)',
    'Y = 20 * tan(0.0099 * X) (cos(0.0099X) ≠ 0)'
  );
  FunctionTextFontColor = clWhite;
  FunctionTextFontSize = 25;
  FunctionTextPositionX = 10;
  FunctionTextPositionY = 400;
  AxisLabelFontColor = clWhite;
  AxisLabelFontSize = 8;
  ArrowSize = 10;
  GridColor = clGray;
  GridSpacing = 50;
  GridLabelFontSize = 8;
  GridLabelPositionY = 420;
  GridLabelPositionX = 10;
  TimerInterval = 40;
  StarMoveStep = 5;
  StarCoordFontColor = clWhite;
  StarCoordFontSize = 25;
  StarCoordPositionX = 10;
  StarCoordPositionY = 450;

implementation

{$R *.lfm}

{ TForm1 }

procedure TForm1.FormCreate(Sender: TObject);
begin
  StarX := -ClientWidth div 2;
  CurrentFunctionIndex := 0;
  Timer1.Interval := TimerInterval;
  Timer1.Enabled := True;
end;

procedure TForm1.FormPaint(Sender: TObject);
var
  StarY: Integer;
begin
  Canvas.Brush.Color := clBlack;
  Canvas.FillRect(ClientRect);
  DrawGrid;
```

```
    DrawAxes;
    DrawFunctionText;

    StarY := CalculateY(StarX) + (ClientHeight div 2);
    DrawStar(StarX + (ClientWidth div 2), StarY, StarSize,
StarColor, StarLineWidth);
    DrawStarCoordinates(StarX, StarY);
end;

procedure TForm1.Timer1Timer(Sender: TObject);
begin
    Inc(StarX, StarMoveStep);
    if StarX > ClientWidth div 2 then
    begin
        StarX := -ClientWidth div 2;
        CurrentFunctionIndex := (CurrentFunctionIndex + 1) mod
Length(GraphFunctions);
    end;
    Invalidate;
end;

procedure TForm1.DrawStar(const CenterX, CenterY, Size:
Integer;
                          const LineColor: TColor; const
LineWidth: Integer);
var
    Points: array[0..9] of TPoint;
    i: Integer;
    Angle: Double;
begin
    for i := 0 to 4 do
    begin
        Angle := -Pi / 2 + (i * 2 * Pi / 5);
        Points[i * 2].X := CenterX + Round(Size * Cos(Angle));
        Points[i * 2].Y := CenterY + Round(Size * Sin(Angle));

        Angle := -Pi / 2 + ((i + 0.5) * 2 * Pi / 5);
        Points[i * 2 + 1].X := CenterX + Round(Size * Cos(Angle)
/ 2);
        Points[i * 2 + 1].Y := CenterY + Round(Size * Sin(Angle) /
2);
    end;

    Canvas.Pen.Color := LineColor;
    Canvas.Pen.Width := LineWidth;
    Canvas.Brush.Style := bsClear;

    Canvas.MoveTo(Points[0].X, Points[0].Y);
```

```
    for i := 1 to 10 do
    begin
      Canvas.LineTo(Points[i mod 10].X, Points[i mod 10].Y);
    end;
end;

procedure TForm1.DrawAxes;
begin
  Canvas.Pen.Color := clWhite;
  Canvas.Pen.Width := 2;
  Canvas.MoveTo(0, ClientHeight div 2);
  Canvas.LineTo(ClientWidth, ClientHeight div 2);
  Canvas.MoveTo(ClientWidth div 2, 0);
  Canvas.LineTo(ClientWidth div 2, ClientHeight);

  Canvas.Font.Color := AxisLabelFontColor;
  Canvas.Font.Size := AxisLabelFontSize;
  Canvas.TextOut(ClientWidth - 20, ClientHeight div 2 + 5,
'X');
  Canvas.TextOut(ClientWidth div 2 + 5, 5, 'Y');
  Canvas.TextOut(ClientWidth div 2 + 5, ClientHeight div 2 +
5, 'O');
end;

procedure TForm1.DrawGrid;
var
  i: Integer;
  GridX, GridY: Integer;
begin
  Canvas.Pen.Color := GridColor;
  Canvas.Pen.Width := 1;
  Canvas.Font.Size := GridLabelFontSize;

  for i := -ClientWidth div 2 to ClientWidth div 2 do
  begin
    if (i mod GridSpacing = 0) and (i <> 0) then
    begin
      GridX := i + (ClientWidth div 2);
      Canvas.MoveTo(GridX, 0);
      Canvas.LineTo(GridX, ClientHeight);
      Canvas.TextOut(GridX - 10, ClientHeight div 2 + 5,
IntToStr(i));
    end;
  end;

  for i := -ClientHeight div 2 to ClientHeight div 2 do
  begin
    if (i mod GridSpacing = 0) and (i <> 0) then
```

```
      begin
        GridY := i + (ClientHeight div 2);
        Canvas.MoveTo(0, GridY);
        Canvas.LineTo(ClientWidth, GridY);
        Canvas.TextOut(ClientWidth div 2 + 5, GridY - 10,
IntToStr(-i));
      end;
    end;
end;

procedure TForm1.DrawFunctionText;
begin
  Canvas.Font.Color := FunctionTextFontColor;
  Canvas.Font.Size := FunctionTextFontSize;
  Canvas.TextOut(FunctionTextPositionX,
FunctionTextPositionY, FunctionTexts[CurrentFunctionIndex]);
end;

procedure TForm1.DrawStarCoordinates(X, Y: Integer);
var
  CoordText: String;
begin
  Y := -Y + (ClientHeight div 2); // convert math coordinate
plane
  Canvas.Font.Color := StarCoordFontColor;
  Canvas.Font.Size := StarCoordFontSize;
  CoordText := Format('(X=%d, Y=%d)', [X, Y]);
  Canvas.TextOut(StarCoordPositionX, StarCoordPositionY,
CoordText);
end;

function TForm1.CalculateY(X: Integer): Integer;
var
  XValue: Double;
begin

  case GraphFunctions[CurrentFunctionIndex] of
    0: Result := Round(0.0077 * Power(X, 2)-150);
    1: Result := Round(Abs(0.5 * X +100 ));
    2: Result := Round(150 * Sin(0.03 * X));
    3: if X <> 0 then
        //Result := Round(7000 / X)
        Result := Round(9000 / X)

      else
        Result := 0;
    4: if Cos(2 + X) <> 0 then
```

```
            Result := Round(10*Sin(0.0099 * X) / Cos(0.0099 *
X))
        else
            Result := 0;
    else
        Result := 0;
    end;
    Result := - Result; // From1's Y direction is downward
end;

end.
```

Summary for Beginners

This program uses only Form1 and Timer1.

Timer1:

Acts like a clock, updating the star's position every 40 milliseconds.

Star Movement:

The star moves horizontally across the form, and its vertical position changes according to mathematical functions.

Mathematical Functions:

The program uses different functions (like sine, quadratic) to determine how the star moves up and down.

Dynamic Display:

As the star moves, the form is continuously updated to show its new position, creating an animation effect.

One more step detail explanation

Understanding the Timer1 Component and Star Movement Logic
Timer1 Component:

In Lazarus, a TTimer component is used to execute code at regular intervals.

In your program, Timer1 is this component. It's set up to trigger an event repeatedly after a specified interval.

The interval is defined by Timer1.Interval, which is set to 40 milliseconds in the FormCreate procedure. This means the Timer1Timer event will be called every 40 milliseconds.

Timer1Timer Event:

The Timer1Timer procedure is where the movement of the star is controlled.

Each time this event is triggered, the program calculates the new position of the star based on a mathematical function.
The star's horizontal position (StarX) is incremented by a constant value (StarMoveStep, set to 5) on each timer tick. This creates a continuous movement effect.

Cycling Through Mathematical Functions:

The program includes an array GraphFunctions that represents different mathematical functions.
CurrentFunctionIndex is used to keep track of which function is currently being used to calculate the star's vertical position (StarY).

When the star reaches the edge of the form (either left or right), CurrentFunctionIndex is incremented, and the program switches to the next function in the array.

CalculateY Function:

The CalculateY function is crucial for determining the star's vertical position based on the current mathematical function.

It takes the current StarX position, adjusts it based on the GraphScale, and then applies the selected mathematical function to calculate StarY.
The mathematical function used depends on the value of CurrentFunctionIndex.

Redrawing the Form:

After updating the star's position, Invalidate is called at the end of the Timer1Timer procedure.
Invalidate forces the form to be repainted, which triggers the FormPaint event.
During the FormPaint event, the updated position of the star is drawn on the form, along with the grid, axes, and function text.

Changing the Speed of the Star's Movement in Lazarus

To adjust the speed of the star's movement in the Lazarus program, you need to change the value of the TimerInterval constant in the program's code.

Contrary to what might be expected, changes made to the Interval property in the Object Inspector will not affect the speed if the interval is explicitly set in the code.

How to Modify the TimerInterval

Find the Constant:

In your program, look for the const section, which is usually at the beginning of your unit (e.g., Unit1.pas). Here, you will find a line like TimerInterval = 40;.

Change the Value:

To increase the speed of the star's movement, reduce the TimerInterval value. For example, changing it from 40 to 20 will make the star move faster. This is because the Timer1Timer event, which updates the star's position, will be triggered more frequently.

Recompile the Program:

After changing the value, recompile your program. When you run it again, you will notice that the star moves across the screen at the new, adjusted speed.

Example:

Change the line in your code from:

TimerInterval = **40**;

to:

TimerInterval = **20**;

This change will cause the star to move twice as fast as before.

By modifying the TimerInterval constant in the code, you can effectively control the animation speed of the star in your Lazarus application.

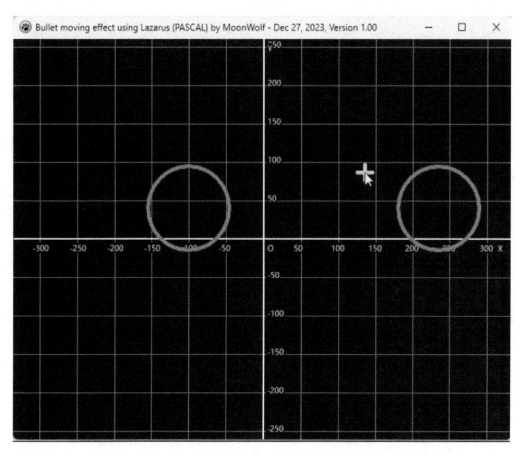

Bullet moving effect using Lazarus (PASCAL) by MoonWolf - Dec 27, 2023, Version 1.00

When click anywhere in XY Coordinate plane, + mark will be appeared at the point. Two bullets from right and left goes to the + mark at the same time by reducing their size.

Until Chapter 6, most of the contents were purely mathematics. That is useful anyone who like mathematics. Or that can be used for educational purposes for teachers and students.

120

Now, from this Chapter7, the contents are mainly for game developer. The game related logical detail is going to be discussed.

In this Chapter, I am going to tell you how to make visual effect of bullet moving towards clicking point of mouse. The visual effect seems very simple; however, the logic is not simple. You need to carefully read the explanation.

Mouse Click Behavior in the Program

Initial State:

Before any mouse click, bullets are positioned off-screen at the left and right edges at Y=0 (the middle of the Y-axis), but they are not visible.

On Mouse Click:

When the user clicks on the form, a "+" mark appears at the clicked location, indicating the target position.

Bullet Movement:

In response to the click, bullets from both the left and right sides start moving towards the "+" mark. As they travel, their radius gradually decreases, creating a dynamic visual effect.

Simultaneous Arrival:

The movement of the bullets is calculated so that they reach the "+" mark at approximately the same time. This synchronized arrival enhances the visual impact of the effect.

Visual Effect:

The entire sequence creates an engaging visual effect, where the bullets seem to be drawn to the clicked point, converging on it from opposite sides of the screen.

Detailed Explanation of the Program's Logic

Mouse Click Event (FormMouseDown)

When the user clicks on the form, this event is triggered.
The clicked coordinates (X, Y) are captured and set as the target
location (TargetX, TargetY) for the bullets.
At this moment, the initial positions and the target position for
the bullets are determined.

Calculation of Bullet Movement

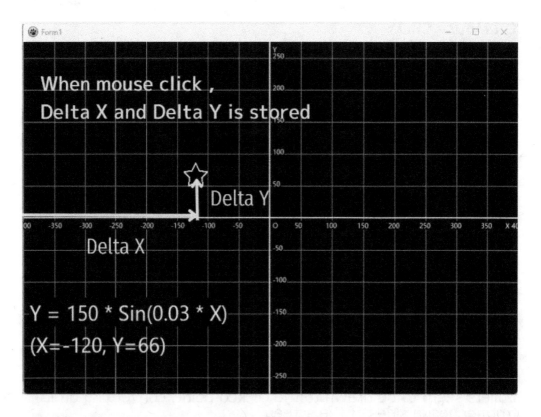

The distance (delta X and delta Y) between the initial positions of
the left and right bullets and the target position is calculated.
This distance is divided by the total number of frames
(TotalFrames) to determine the movement per frame for each
bullet.

This calculation ensures that the bullets move towards the target at a consistent speed.

Size Adjustment of the Bullets

Simultaneously, the radius of the bullets is set to gradually decrease.
The change in radius from the initial (InitialBulletRadius) to the final radius (FinalBulletRadius) is divided by TotalFrames to determine the reduction in radius per frame.
As a result, the bullets gradually decrease in size as they move towards the target.

Timer Event (Timer1Timer)

Each time the timer event occurs, the position and size of the bullets are updated.
The bullets' positions are updated based on the calculated movement per frame (delta X and delta Y).
The radius of each bullet is also updated based on the calculated reduction per frame.

Visual Effect and Logical Complexity

The logic ensures that the bullets move towards the target at a steady pace, shrinking in size as they approach.
The bullets start from the left and right edges of the screen and converge towards the clicked point.

The calculated movement and size reduction per frame create a visually appealing effect where the bullets appear to be dynamically moving and shrinking.

For beginners, understanding this logic can be challenging as it involves coordinate calculation, frame-based movement, and dynamic resizing of graphical elements.

The program effectively demonstrates how user interaction (mouse click) can be translated into a sophisticated visual response using mathematical calculations and graphical updates.

This program, while visually simple, incorporates a complex logic that elegantly handles user interaction and dynamic visual rendering, making it an excellent example for educational purposes, especially for beginners learning about graphical programming and event-driven logic in Lazarus (Free Pascal).

Relationship Between TotalFrames and Timer1.Interval

TotalFrames:

This constant represents the total number of frames that the animation (movement of the bullet) will be spread across. It defines the length of the animation sequence.

Timer1.Interval:

This property of the Timer1 component specifies the interval (in milliseconds) at which the Timer1Timer event is triggered. Each trigger represents a single frame in the context of the animation.

How They Work Together

The Timer1.Interval determines how often the screen is updated. For example, if Timer1.Interval is set to 40 milliseconds, the Timer1Timer event (and thus the screen update) occurs every 40 milliseconds.

TotalFrames dictates how many of these updates (or frames) are needed for the bullet to complete its movement from the starting point to the target point.

The combination of Timer1.Interval and TotalFrames controls the speed and duration of the bullet's movement. A lower TotalFrames with a fixed Timer1.Interval results in a faster animation, as the bullet moves a greater distance with each frame.

Example
If Timer1.Interval is 40 milliseconds and TotalFrames is set to 20, the entire animation from start to finish will take 800 milliseconds (40 ms/frame * 20 frames = 800 ms).

In summary, TotalFrames sets the length of the animation in terms of frames, while Timer1.Interval determines the time between each frame. Together, they control the timing and pacing of the bullet's movement animation in the program.

What need to be done

[1] Copy the code to your code editor
[2] Object inspector setting(link the ivent to the source code)
    From1 > onCreate , onPaint, onMouseDown
    Timer1 > onTimer
[3] Compile the program
[4] Run the program

```
unit Unit1;

{$mode objfpc}{$H+}

interface

uses
    Classes, SysUtils, Forms, Controls, Graphics, ExtCtrls, Math;

type
    TForm1 = class(TForm)
        Timer1: TTimer; // Timer for continuous updates during
gameplay.
        procedure FormCreate(Sender: TObject); // Called when
the form is created.
        procedure FormPaint(Sender: TObject); // Called for
drawing on the form.
        procedure Timer1Timer(Sender: TObject); // Called on
each timer tick.
        procedure FormMouseDown(Sender: TObject; Button:
TMouseButton;
            Shift: TShiftState; X, Y: Integer); // Called when a
mouse button is clicked.
    private
```

```
    // Variables to manage the bullets' state and position.
    BulletActiveLeft, BulletActiveRight: Boolean;
    BulletXLeft, BulletYLeft: Integer;
    BulletXRight, BulletYRight: Integer;

    // Variables for scoring and target positioning.
    TargetX, TargetY: Integer;
    Score: Integer;
    ShowTargetMark: Boolean;

    // Additional variables for dynamic bullet behavior.
    BulletRadiusLeft, BulletRadiusRight: Integer; // Radius of
the bullets.
    DeltaXLeft, DeltaYLeft: Integer; // Movement per frame for
left bullet.
    DeltaXRight, DeltaYRight: Integer; // Movement per frame
for right bullet.
    DeltaRadiusLeft, DeltaRadiusRight: Integer; // Radius
reduction per frame.

    procedure DrawAxes;
    procedure DrawGrid;
    procedure DrawBullet(const X, Y, Radius: Integer);
    procedure DrawTargetMark(const X, Y: Integer);

  public
  end;

var
  Form1: TForm1;

const

  // Additional constants for UI elements.

  AxisLabelFontColor = clWhite;
  AxisLabelFontSize = 8;
  ArrowSize = 10;
  GridColor = clGray;
  GridSpacing = 50;
  GridLabelFontSize = 8;

  TimerInterval = 40;

  // Constants for bullet dynamics and game scoring.
  InitialBulletRadius = 50; // Initial radius of the bullets.
  FinalBulletRadius = 10;    // Final radius of the bullets.
```

```
  BulletShrinkRate = 5;        // Rate at which bullets shrink.
  BulletSpeed = 5;             // Speed of the bullets.
  HitTolerance = 10;           // Tolerance for hit detection.
  ScoreHit = 100;              // Points awarded for a hit.
  ScoreMiss = -10;             // Points deducted for a miss.
  BulletColor = clRed;         // Color of the bullets.
  BulletBorderWidth = 5;       // Width of the bullet outline.
  TargetHitTolerance = 15;     // Tolerance for hitting the target.
  TargetMarkColor = clLime;    // Color of the target marker.
  TargetMarkSize = 10;         // Size of the target marker.
  TargetMarkAdjustX = 0;       // X-coordinate adjustment for
target marker.
  TargetMarkAdjustY = 0;       // Y-coordinate adjustment for
target marker.
  TotalFrames = 20;            // Number of frames for bullet
movement.


implementation

{$R *.lfm}

{ TForm1 }

procedure TForm1.FormCreate(Sender: TObject);
begin
  Caption := 'Bullet moving effect using Lazarus (PASCAL) by
MoonWolf - Dec 27, 2023, Version 1.00';
  Timer1.Interval := TimerInterval;
  Timer1.Enabled := True;
  BulletActiveLeft := False;
  BulletActiveRight := False;
  Score := 0;
end;

procedure TForm1.FormPaint(Sender: TObject);
begin
  Canvas.Brush.Color := clBlack;
  Canvas.FillRect(ClientRect);
  DrawGrid;
  DrawAxes;

  if BulletActiveLeft then
    DrawBullet(BulletXLeft, BulletYLeft, BulletRadiusLeft);
  if BulletActiveRight then
    DrawBullet(BulletXRight, BulletYRight, BulletRadiusRight);
  if ShowTargetMark then
```

```
      DrawTargetMark(TargetX + TargetMarkAdjustX, TargetY +
TargetMarkAdjustY);
end;

procedure TForm1.Timer1Timer(Sender: TObject);
begin

  // Adjusting the movement of the left bullet
  if BulletActiveLeft then
  begin
    BulletXLeft := BulletXLeft + DeltaXLeft;
    BulletYLeft := BulletYLeft + DeltaYLeft;
    BulletRadiusLeft := Max(BulletRadiusLeft - DeltaRadiusLeft,
10);

    if (Abs(BulletXLeft - TargetX) <= TargetHitTolerance) and
       (Abs(BulletYLeft - TargetY) <= TargetHitTolerance)
then
    begin
      BulletActiveLeft := False;
      BulletXLeft := TargetX;
      BulletYLeft := TargetY;
      BulletRadiusLeft := 10;
      if not BulletActiveRight then
        ShowTargetMark := False;
    end;
  end;

  // Adjusting the movement of the right bullet
  if BulletActiveRight then
  begin
    BulletXRight := BulletXRight + DeltaXRight;
    BulletYRight := BulletYRight + DeltaYRight;
    BulletRadiusRight := Max(BulletRadiusRight -
DeltaRadiusRight, 10);

    if (Abs(BulletXRight - TargetX) <= TargetHitTolerance) and
       (Abs(BulletYRight - TargetY) <= TargetHitTolerance)
then
    begin
      BulletActiveRight := False;
      BulletXRight := TargetX;
      BulletYRight := TargetY;
      BulletRadiusRight := 10;
      if not BulletActiveLeft then
        ShowTargetMark := False;
    end;
  end;
```

```
   Invalidate; // Redrawing the screen
end;

procedure TForm1.FormMouseDown(Sender: TObject; Button:
TMouseButton;
   Shift: TShiftState; X, Y: Integer);
const
   InitialBulletRadius = 100; // Initial radius of the bullets.
   FinalBulletRadius = 10;     // Final radius of the bullets.
   TotalFrames = 10;             // Number of frames for bullet
movement.
begin
   TargetX := X; // Set the target X-coordinate to the clicked
position.
   TargetY := Y; // Set the target Y-coordinate to the clicked
position.

   // Initialize the left bullet at the left edge of the form.
   BulletActiveLeft := True;
   BulletXLeft := 0; // Start from the left edge.
   BulletYLeft := Form1.Height div 2; // Start from the vertical
center.
   BulletRadiusLeft := InitialBulletRadius; // Set the initial
radius.
   DeltaRadiusLeft := (InitialBulletRadius - FinalBulletRadius)
div TotalFrames; // Set radius decrease per frame.
   DeltaXLeft := (TargetX - BulletXLeft) div TotalFrames; // Set
horizontal movement per frame.
   DeltaYLeft := (TargetY - BulletYLeft) div TotalFrames; // Set
vertical movement per frame.

   // Initialize the right bullet at the right edge of the form.
   BulletActiveRight := True;
   BulletXRight := Form1.Width; // Start from the right edge.
   BulletYRight := Form1.Height div 2; // Start from the vertical
center.
   BulletRadiusRight := InitialBulletRadius; // Set the initial
radius.
   DeltaRadiusRight := (InitialBulletRadius - FinalBulletRadius)
div TotalFrames; // Set radius decrease per frame.
   DeltaXRight := (TargetX - BulletXRight) div TotalFrames; //
Set horizontal movement per frame.
   DeltaYRight := (TargetY - BulletYRight) div TotalFrames; //
Set vertical movement per frame.

   ShowTargetMark := True; // Show the target mark at the
clicked position.
```

```
end;

// Draws coordinate axes on the form.
procedure TForm1.DrawAxes;
begin
   // Drawing the X and Y axes in white.
   Canvas.Pen.Color := clWhite;
   Canvas.Pen.Width := 2;
   Canvas.MoveTo(0, ClientHeight div 2);
   Canvas.LineTo(ClientWidth, ClientHeight div 2);
   Canvas.MoveTo(ClientWidth div 2, 0);
   Canvas.LineTo(ClientWidth div 2, ClientHeight);

   // Labeling the axes.
   Canvas.Font.Color := AxisLabelFontColor;
   Canvas.Font.Size := AxisLabelFontSize;
   Canvas.TextOut(ClientWidth - 20, ClientHeight div 2 + 5,
'X');
   Canvas.TextOut(ClientWidth div 2 + 5, 5, 'Y');
   Canvas.TextOut(ClientWidth div 2 + 5, ClientHeight div 2 +
5, 'O');
end;

// Draws the grid on the form.
procedure TForm1.DrawGrid;
var
   i: Integer;
   GridX, GridY: Integer;
begin
   // Setting the grid color and line width.
   Canvas.Pen.Color := GridColor;
   Canvas.Pen.Width := 1;
   Canvas.Font.Size := GridLabelFontSize;

   // Drawing grid lines along the X-axis and labeling them.
   for i := -ClientWidth div 2 to ClientWidth div 2 do
   begin
     if (i mod GridSpacing = 0) and (i <> 0) then
     begin
       GridX := i + (ClientWidth div 2);
       Canvas.MoveTo(GridX, 0);
       Canvas.LineTo(GridX, ClientHeight);
       Canvas.TextOut(GridX - 10, ClientHeight div 2 + 5,
IntToStr(i));
     end;
   end;

   // Drawing grid lines along the Y-axis and labeling them.
```

```pascal
    for i := -ClientHeight div 2 to ClientHeight div 2 do
    begin
      if (i mod GridSpacing = 0) and (i <> 0) then
      begin
        GridY := i + (ClientHeight div 2);
        Canvas.MoveTo(0, GridY);
        Canvas.LineTo(ClientWidth, GridY);
        Canvas.TextOut(ClientWidth div 2 + 5, GridY - 10,
IntToStr(-i));
      end;
    end;
end;

// Draws a bullet at the specified position with the given radius.
procedure TForm1.DrawBullet(const X, Y, Radius: Integer);
begin
  // Setting the color and border width for the bullet.
  Canvas.Pen.Color := BulletColor;
  Canvas.Pen.Width := BulletBorderWidth;
  Canvas.Brush.Style := bsClear;

  // Drawing the bullet as an ellipse.
  Canvas.Ellipse(X - Radius, Y - Radius, X + Radius, Y +
Radius);
end;

// Draws a target mark at the specified position.
procedure TForm1.DrawTargetMark(const X, Y: Integer);
begin
  // Setting the color for the target mark.
  Canvas.Pen.Color := TargetMarkColor;

  // Drawing horizontal and vertical lines to represent the
target mark.
  Canvas.MoveTo(X - TargetMarkSize, Y);
  Canvas.LineTo(X + TargetMarkSize, Y);
  Canvas.MoveTo(X, Y - TargetMarkSize);
  Canvas.LineTo(X, Y + TargetMarkSize);
end;

end.
```

Detailed Explanation of Bullet Movement Logic

Initial State of Bullets

The left and right bullets are initially positioned off-screen at the left and right edges of the screen, respectively, at Y=0 (middle of the Y-axis).

They remain invisible and in standby mode until a mouse click occurs.

Mouse Click Event and Target Mark

When the user clicks on any position on the screen, a "+" mark appears at that location. This event is handled in the **FormMouseDown** procedure.

The clicked position becomes the target (**TargetX**, **TargetY**) for the bullets.

Calculating the Delta Values

In **FormMouseDown**, the difference between the target position and the bullet's initial position is calculated.

DeltaX for the left bullet is computed as **TargetX - BulletXLeft**. **DeltaY** for the left bullet is computed as **TargetY - BulletYLeft**.

These calculations determine how much the bullet needs to move horizontally and vertically to reach the target.

Movement and Size Adjustment per Frame

In the **Timer1Timer** procedure, the movement towards the target is executed frame by frame.

DeltaX and **DeltaY** are divided by the total number of frames (**TotalFrames**) to determine the movement per frame.

The bullet's X and Y positions are updated in each frame, moving it closer to the target.

Simultaneously, the bullet's radius is reduced in each frame to create a shrinking effect.

Arrival and Visual Effect

The **Timer1Timer** procedure also checks if the bullet has sufficiently approached the target position.

If the bullet is close enough to the target (within **TargetHitTolerance**), it is considered to have reached the target.

Summary

The program uses the **FormMouseDown** procedure to set the target and calculate delta values.
The **Timer1Timer** procedure then handles the frame-by-frame movement and size adjustment of the bullets.

This detailed explanation provides insight into the logical flow and specific procedures used in the program to create a dynamic and visually engaging effect in response to user interaction.

In this section, we will delve into the topic of hit detection. No matter how visually stunning a game may be, if the hit detection is not meticulously crafted, the game can lose its appeal and become unenjoyable. The hit detection mechanism discussed here is a crucial and central aspect of the gameplay.

It not only ensures fairness and challenge but also significantly contributes to the overall player experience. A well-implemented hit detection system is key to making the game engaging and rewarding.

1. Hit Detection Logic

The hit detection logic in the game is crucial for determining whether the player's action (shooting bullets) successfully hits the target (the star). This logic is implemented as follows:

When bullets are active and moving towards the target, their positions are continuously updated.

Once the bullets reach the vicinity of the target, the program checks if the bullets' coordinates are within a certain tolerance range of the target's coordinates.

This tolerance range is defined to allow a slight margin of error, making the game fair and enjoyable.

If the bullets' coordinates fall within this range, it's considered a hit; otherwise, it's a miss.

2. Visual Representation of "Nice Hit!"

Upon a successful hit, a visual effect is triggered to enhance player feedback and satisfaction. This effect is described as:

When a hit is detected, the message "Nice Hit!" appears on the screen, specifically below the position of the star.

Initially, this message is displayed in a large font size to catch the player's attention.

Over a brief period (around 0.5 seconds), the font size of the message gradually decreases, creating a dynamic visual effect.

This diminishing effect of the message size visually represents the fleeting nature of the successful moment, adding to the game's excitement.

3. Score Increment

Scoring is a fundamental aspect of the game, providing motivation and a sense of achievement. The scoring mechanism works as follows:

Each time the player hits the target, a predefined number of points are added to the total score.

This increment in score is immediately reflected in the game's user interface, allowing the player to see their progress in real-time.

The scoring system is simple yet effective, encouraging players to aim accurately and improve their skills.

These three components—hit detection, visual feedback, and scoring—work together to create an engaging and rewarding gameplay experience. They are essential for keeping the player engaged and motivated throughout the game.

```
// Timer1Timer procedure
procedure TForm1.Timer1Timer(Sender: TObject);
begin
   ...
   // Adjusting the movement of the right bullet
   if BulletActiveRight then
   begin
      ...
      if (Abs(BulletXRight - TargetX) <= TargetHitTolerance) and
         (Abs(BulletYRight - TargetY) <= TargetHitTolerance)
then
         begin
            BulletActiveRight := False;
            BulletXRight := TargetX;
            BulletYRight := TargetY;
            BulletRadiusRight := 10;
            if not BulletActiveLeft then
               ShowTargetMark := False;
         end;
   end;
   ...
end;
```

Hit detection code

Detailed Explanation of Variables in Hit Detection Logic

BulletActiveRight:

This boolean variable indicates whether the right bullet is currently active in the game. An active bullet is one that is in motion towards the target.

139

If BulletActiveRight is True, it means the right bullet is currently moving and can potentially hit the target.

I made hit detection with only right bullet because both bullets right and left come to the clicking point at the same time and at the same size.

BulletXRight, BulletYRight:

These integer variables represent the current X and Y coordinates of the right bullet on the screen. As the bullet moves, these values are updated to reflect its new position. They are crucial for determining the bullet's location at any given moment.

TargetX, TargetY:

These integers hold the X and Y coordinates of the target (the + mark) that the bullet is aiming to hit. The target's position is set when the player clicks on the screen and remains constant until the next click.

TargetHitTolerance:

This variable defines the tolerance range for a hit. It's a threshold value that determines how close the bullet needs to be to the target coordinates to be considered a hit. A smaller value makes the game more challenging, as the bullet needs to be closer to the target to register as a hit.

ShowTargetMark:

A boolean variable that controls the visibility of the target mark (+ sign) on the screen. When set to True, the target mark is visible, indicating where the player has clicked. It's hidden once the bullets have reached their destination or when no target is currently active.

In-Depth Analysis of Hit Detection Logic

The hit detection logic is encapsulated within the Timer1Timer procedure, specifically in the section handling the right bullet's movement. This logic is executed on every tick of the timer, ensuring continuous monitoring of the bullet's position relative to the target.

Bullet Movement and Position Check:

The first step involves updating the bullet's position (BulletXRight and BulletYRight) based on its trajectory towards the target. This trajectory is previously calculated when the player clicks on the screen to set the target.

Hit Detection Condition:

The core of the hit detection logic lies in the conditional statement:

```
if (Abs(BulletXRight - TargetX) <= TargetHitTolerance) and
    (Abs(BulletYRight - TargetY) <= TargetHitTolerance) then
```

This condition checks whether the bullet is within a specified range (TargetHitTolerance) of the target coordinates (TargetX, TargetY). The Abs function calculates the absolute difference between the bullet's current position and the target, ensuring a positive value for comparison.

141

Bullet and Target Interaction:

Upon satisfying the hit detection condition, several actions are triggered:

The bullet is marked as inactive (BulletActiveRight := False), stopping its movement.
The bullet's position is set to the target's coordinates, visually representing a hit.
The bullet's radius is reset, preparing it for the next shot.

Visibility of Target Mark:

The ShowTargetMark variable is set to False if there are no active bullets left. This hides the target mark from the screen, indicating the completion of the current shot.

Simultaneous Arrival of Bullets:

It's important to note that the hit detection for the right bullet is part of a synchronized mechanism with the left bullet. Both bullets are designed to reach the target simultaneously, creating a visually appealing effect. This synchronization is achieved through careful calculation of each bullet's trajectory and speed.

This detailed breakdown of the hit detection logic for the right bullet provides a deeper insight into the game's mechanics. It highlights the precision and considerations involved in ensuring a responsive and engaging gameplay experience. Understanding this logic is crucial for grasping the intricacies of game development, particularly in aspects related to player interaction and feedback.

```
// FormPaint procedure
procedure TForm1.FormPaint(Sender: TObject);
begin
  ...
  // Hit message
  if ShowHitMessage then
  begin
    CurrentFontSize := Max(12, InitialMessageFontSize *
HitMessageTimer div MaxHitMessageTimer);
    Canvas.Font.Size := CurrentFontSize;
    Canvas.Font.Color := clWhite;
    Canvas.TextOut(StarX + (ClientWidth div 2) -
CurrentFontSize * 2, StarY + 20, 'Nice Hit!');
  end;
end;
```

Hit Message code

To explain the "Nice Hit!" message display logic in your Lazarus Pascal program, let's first look at the relevant const and private declarations, and then delve into the detailed logic of how the message is displayed and dynamically adjusted.

Relevant Declarations:

private section:

ShowHitMessage: Boolean;

A boolean flag to control the visibility of the "Nice Hit!" message.

HitMessageTimer: Integer;

A timer variable that counts down the frames for which the hit message is displayed.

StarX, StarY: Integer;
Variables to track the star's position, used for positioning the message.

const section:

HitMessageDuration = 9;

The number of frames the hit message is displayed (0.7 seconds at 40ms per frame).

InitialMessageFontSize = 120;

The initial font size of the hit message.

MaxHitMessageTimer = 15;

The maximum duration for the message display in frames.

Display Logic of "Nice Hit!" Message:

When a hit is detected, **ShowHitMessage** is set to **True**, and **HitMessageTimer** is initialized to **HitMessageDuration**.

In the **FormPaint** procedure, if **ShowHitMessage** is **True**, the message is displayed.

The font size of the message starts large

(**InitialMessageFontSize**) and decreases each frame.

144

The size reduction is calculated using **CurrentFontSize :=
Max(12, InitialMessageFontSize * HitMessageTimer div
MaxHitMessageTimer);**

This formula ensures that the font size decreases over time but
does not go below a readable minimum (12 in this case).

The message is displayed below the star **(StarY + 20)** and
centered horizontally based on the star's position **(StarX +
(ClientWidth div 2) - CurrentFontSize * 2).**

Each frame, **HitMessageTimer** is decremented, reducing the
font size until the message disappears.

This dynamic change in font size creates a visual effect where
the "Nice Hit!" message appears to burst and then shrink away,
adding a visually engaging element to the game. The constants
HitMessageDuration, InitialMessageFontSize, and
MaxHitMessageTimer allow for easy adjustments to the
duration and visual impact of this effect, catering to different
preferences or gameplay styles.

Overview:

In the game, the player's score is updated based on successful hit detection. When a player successfully hits a target, their score increases, and conversely, it decreases on a miss. This scoring system is displayed in real-time on the top left of the screen using the Canvas.

Relevant Variables and Constants:

Score:

A private variable that holds the current score of the player.

ScoreHit:

A constant that defines the points added to the score for a successful hit.

ScoreMiss:

A constant that defines the points subtracted from the score for a miss.

HitTolerance:

A constant that determines the acceptable range for a hit to be considered successful.

Logic Explanation:

The game checks if the star's position aligns with the target within the HitTolerance range.

If the star is within this range, it's considered a hit, and ScoreHit points are added to the Score.

If the star is outside this range, it's a miss, and ScoreMiss points are deducted from the Score.

```
// Timer1Timer procedure
procedure TForm1.Timer1Timer(Sender: TObject);
begin
  ...
  // Check if both bullets have stopped moving
  if (not BulletActiveLeft) and (not BulletActiveRight) then
  begin
    // Hit detection logic
    if (Abs(StarX + (ClientWidth div 2) - TargetX) <=
HitTolerance) and
       (Abs(StarY - TargetY) <= HitTolerance) then
      Score := Score + ScoreHit   // Increase score for a hit
    else
      Score := Score + ScoreMiss;   // Decrease score for a
miss
  end;
  ...
end;
```

The **Timer1Timer** procedure is part of the game loop,
continuously checking for game state updates.

The hit detection is performed within this procedure. It calculates
the distance between the star and the target, comparing it
against **HitTolerance**.

Depending on whether this condition is met (a hit) or not (a
miss), the score is updated accordingly.

Displaying the Score:

148

The updated score is displayed on the Canvas, typically in the **FormPaint** procedure, ensuring it's visible in real-time during gameplay.

```
// FormPaint procedure
procedure TForm1.FormPaint(Sender: TObject);
begin
  ...
  Canvas.TextOut(10, 10, 'Score: ' + IntToStr(Score));   //
Displaying the score
  ...
end;
```

This scoring system adds a competitive edge to the game, motivating players to aim accurately and strategize their moves. The real-time score display keeps players informed of their performance, enhancing the gaming experience.

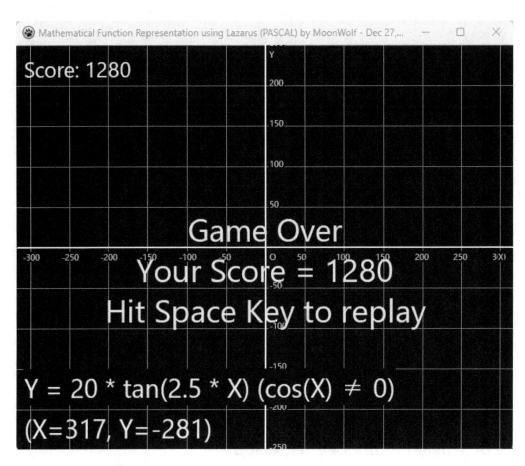

Score: 1280

Game Over

Your Score = 1280

Hit Space Key to replay

Y = 20 * tan(2.5 * X) (cos(X) ≠ 0)

(X=317, Y=-281)

Game Over Screen

In this chapter, I am going to tell you how to judge game over, how to display the text, how to accept space key to replay.

Game Over Process in this program

150

1. Variables Related to Game Over

GameOver: Boolean;

This variable tracks whether the game is in a Game Over state.

2. Constants and Initial Settings

No specific constants related to Game Over were defined.

3. Game Over Condition

Located in procedure TForm1.Timer1Timer(Sender: TObject);
The Game Over condition is triggered when FunctionRepeatCount
reaches a certain threshold (in this case, **>= 2**).

This count is incremented each time the star completes a cycle
across the screen.

Once the condition is met, GameOver is set to True, and the
DisplayGameOverMessage procedure is called. The game's timer
is also stopped.

4. Displaying Game Over Message

procedure TForm1.DisplayGameOverMessage;
This procedure is responsible for displaying the Game Over
message. It sets the font size and color, and positions the text
"Game Over" along with the player's score and a prompt to hit
the space key to replay, centered on the screen.

5. Resetting Game After Game Over

In procedure TForm1.FormKeyDown(Sender: TObject; var Key: Word; Shift: TShiftState);
If the space key is pressed (VK_SPACE) and GameOver is True, the game resets. This includes resetting the score, FunctionRepeatCount, and the GameOver flag. The game's timer is re-enabled.

** When you use VK_SPACE (or any other Virtual Key), you need to write LCLType in uses.

Summary

The Game Over process in this program is primarily managed through the GameOver boolean variable, which is set based on a condition in the Timer1Timer procedure. The display of the Game Over message and the option to restart the game are handled in the DisplayGameOverMessage procedure and FormKeyDown procedures.

```
unit Unit1;

interface

// ... [Other interface declarations]

type
  TForm1 = class(TForm)
    // ... [Other component declarations]
  private
    GameOver: Boolean; // Tracks the game over state
    // ... [Other private declarations]

    procedure DisplayGameOverMessage; // Procedure to
display the game over message

    // ... [Other procedure and function declarations]
  public
    // ... [Public declarations]
  end;

var
  Form1: TForm1;

implementation

{ TForm1 }

procedure TForm1.FormCreate(Sender: TObject);
begin
  // ... [Initialization code]
  GameOver := False; // Initialize Game Over state
end;
```

```
procedure TForm1.Timer1Timer(Sender: TObject);
begin
  // ... [Other timer related code]

  // Check for Game Over condition
  if FunctionRepeatCount >= 2 then
  begin
    GameOver := True; // Set Game Over state
    DisplayGameOverMessage; // Call to display Game Over
message
    Timer1.Enabled := False; // Stop the timer
    Exit; // Exit the procedure
  end;

  // ... [Other timer related code]
end;

procedure TForm1.DisplayGameOverMessage;
begin
  // Set font properties for Game Over message
  Canvas.Font.Size := 30;
  Canvas.Font.Color := clyellow;

  // Display Game Over message and score, centered on the
screen
  Canvas.TextOut((ClientWidth - Canvas.TextWidth('Game
Over')) div 2, (ClientHeight div 2) - 50, 'Game Over');
  Canvas.TextOut((ClientWidth - Canvas.TextWidth('Your
Score = ' + IntToStr(Score))) div 2, ClientHeight div 2, 'Your
Score = ' + IntToStr(Score));
  Canvas.TextOut((ClientWidth - Canvas.TextWidth('Hit Space
Key to replay')) div 2, (ClientHeight div 2) + 50, 'Hit Space Key
to replay');
end;

procedure TForm1.FormKeyDown(Sender: TObject; var Key:
Word; Shift: TShiftState);
begin
  // ... [Other key handling code]

  // Reset game if space key is pressed after Game Over
  if (Key = VK_SPACE) and GameOver then
  begin
    Score := 0;
    FunctionRepeatCount := 0;
    GameOver := False; // Reset Game Over state
    Timer1.Enabled := True; // Re-enable the timer
  end;
```

```
  // ... [Other key handling code]
end;

// ... [Other TForm1 methods]

end.
```

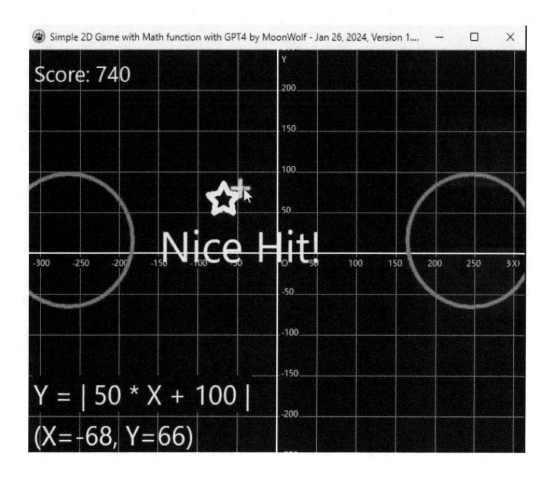

You have learned how to create XY coordinates, drawing start, moving start with math functions, visual effects of bullet, hit judgement, scoring.

ChatGPT4 cannot develop this game at once. Step by step approach is required. The Chapters what I mention before are how I have developed this game.

In this chapter, I integrate them all in one program. I am going to tell you how it works with all of them.

```
//////////////////////////////////////////////////////////////////
//////////////
//////////   //////////////////////////////////////////////////////////////
//////////////
/////
/////      Important Notice:
/////
/////      Do not remove this comment when using this program.
/////      Removing it will result in a copyright infringement.
/////      As long as this comment remains, the author, MoonWolf,
/////      allows you to freely utilize this program.
/////
/////      Usage examples: Personal program study, showing to
/////      friends, presentations at school,
/////      submission as a free assignment during winter or
/////      summer holidays, reference material for graduation
thesis,
/////      teachers demonstrating functions to students using this
program.
/////      You can use it freely without MoonWolf's consent.
/////
/////      The program can be partly modified to
/////      customize the graph shape and more.
/////      Particularly, fine-tuning is possible through
/////      constant definitions in the Const section.
/////
/////      All rights reserved
/////      (c)2024 MoonWolf
/////
/////      Program: Simple 2D Game with Math function assisted
by ChatGPT4
/////      Version: 1.00
/////      Created by: MoonWolf / Assisted by ChatGPT4
/////      Twitter: MoonWolf_001
/////      Development Environment: Window11 + Lazarus 2.2.6
/////      Release Date: January 26, 2024
/////
/////      Remarks:
/////
/////      Lazarus is a programming development environment.
/////      It's a free programming development environment.
/////      The programming language is Pascal.
/////      For programming beginners, it's less difficult than
```

```
unit Unit1;

{$mode objfpc}{$H+}

interface

uses
  Classes, SysUtils, Forms, Controls, Graphics, ExtCtrls, Math,
LCLType, Dialogs;
```

```pascal
type
  // TForm1 is the main form class for the application.
  // It handles all the visual elements and game logic.
  TForm1 = class(TForm)
    Timer1: TTimer; // Timer for continuous updates during
gameplay.
    procedure FormCreate(Sender: TObject); // Called when
the form is created.
    procedure FormKeyDown(Sender: TObject; var Key: Word;
Shift: TShiftState);
    procedure FormPaint(Sender: TObject); // Called for
drawing on the form.
    procedure Timer1Timer(Sender: TObject); // Called on
each timer tick.
    procedure FormMouseDown(Sender: TObject; Button:
TMouseButton;
        Shift: TShiftState; X, Y: Integer); // Called when a
mouse button is clicked.
  private
    ShowHitMessage: Boolean; // Whether to display the hit
message
    HitMessageTimer: Integer; // Timer to manage the display
duration of the hit message
    FunctionRepeatCount: Integer; // Variable to track the
number of times a function is repeated
    GameOver: Boolean; // Tracks the game over state

    // Variables to track the star's position and current
mathematical function.
    StarX, StarY: Integer;
    CurrentFunctionIndex: Integer;

    // Variables to manage the bullets' state and position.
    BulletActiveLeft, BulletActiveRight: Boolean;
    BulletXLeft, BulletYLeft: Integer;
    BulletXRight, BulletYRight: Integer;

    // Variables for scoring and target positioning.
    TargetX, TargetY: Integer;
    Score: Integer;
    ShowTargetMark: Boolean;

    // Additional variables for dynamic bullet behavior.
    BulletRadiusLeft, BulletRadiusRight: Integer; // Radius of
the bullets.
    DeltaXLeft, DeltaYLeft: Integer; // Movement per frame for
left bullet.
```

```pascal
      DeltaXRight, DeltaYRight: Integer; // Movement per frame
for right bullet.
      DeltaRadiusLeft, DeltaRadiusRight: Integer; // Radius
reduction per frame.

      InitialMessageFontSize: Integer; // Initial font size of the
message
      MaxHitMessageTimer: Integer; // Maximum display time of
the message
      FirstClickOccurred: Boolean; // Variable to track whether
the first mouse click has occurred

      // Procedures for drawing various elements on the form.
      procedure DisplayGameOverMessage;
      procedure DrawStar(const CenterX, CenterY, Size: Integer;
                    const LineColor: TColor; const
LineWidth: Integer);
      procedure DrawAxes;
      procedure DrawGrid;
      procedure DrawFunctionText;
      procedure DrawStarCoordinates(X, Y: Integer);
      procedure DrawBullet(const X, Y, Radius: Integer);
      procedure DrawScore;
      procedure DrawTargetMark(const X, Y: Integer);

      // Function to calculate the Y-coordinate based on a
mathematical function.
      function CalculateY(X: Integer): Integer;
   public
   end;

var
   Form1: TForm1;

const
   // Constants for graphical elements and game mechanics.
   StarSize = 20; // Size of the star.
   StarColor = clYellow; // Color of the star.
   StarLineWidth = 7; // Width of the star's outline.
   GraphScale = 100; // Scaling factor for graphing functions.

   // Array of mathematical functions represented in the game.
   GraphFunctions: array[0..4] of Integer = (0, 1, 2, 3, 4);
   FunctionTexts: array[0..4] of string = (
      'Y = 0.0077 * X^2 - 150', // Quadratic function.
      'Y = |0.5 * X + 100|', // Absolute value function.
      'Y = 150 * Sin(0.03 * X)', // Sine function.
      'Y = 9000 / X (X ≠ 0)', // Inverse function.
```

```
    'Y = 10 * tan(0.0099 * X) (cos(0.0099X) ≠ 0)' // Tangent
function.
  );

  // Additional constants for UI elements.
  FunctionTextFontColor = clWhite; // Font color for displaying
function text.
  FunctionTextFontSize = 25; // Font size for displaying
function text.
  FunctionTextPositionX = 10; // X-coordinate for function text
position.
  FunctionTextPositionY = 400; // Y-coordinate for function
text position.
  AxisLabelFontColor = clWhite; // Font color for axis labels.
  AxisLabelFontSize = 8; // Font size for axis labels.
  ArrowSize = 10; // Size of the axis arrows.
  GridColor = clGray; // Color of the grid lines.
  GridSpacing = 50; // Spacing between grid lines.
  GridLabelFontSize = 8; // Font size for grid labels.
  TimerInterval = 40; // Interval for the game timer.
  StarMoveStep = 5; // Movement step size for the star.
  StarCoordFontColor = clWhite; // Font color for star
coordinates.
  StarCoordFontSize = 25; // Font size for star coordinates.
  StarCoordPositionX = 10; // X-coordinate for star coordinates
position.
  StarCoordPositionY = 450; // Y-coordinate for star
coordinates position.
  HitMessageDuration = 14; // Number of frames to display
the hit message (0.7 seconds).
  InitialBulletRadius = 50; // Initial radius of the bullets.
  FinalBulletRadius = 10; // Final radius of the bullets.
  BulletShrinkRate = 5; // Rate at which bullets shrink.
  BulletSpeed = 5; // Speed of the bullets.
  HitTolerance = 15; // Tolerance for hit detection.
  ScoreHit = 100; // Points awarded for a hit.
  ScoreMiss = -10; // Points deducted for a miss.
  BulletColor = clRed; // Color of the bullets.
  BulletBorderWidth = 5; // Width of the bullet outline.
  TargetHitTolerance = 15; // Tolerance for hitting the target.
  TargetMarkColor = clLime; // Color of the target marker.
  TargetMarkSize = 10; // Size of the target marker.
  TargetMarkAdjustX = 0; // X-coordinate adjustment for
target marker.
  TargetMarkAdjustY = 0; // Y-coordinate adjustment for
target marker.
  TotalFrames = 20; // Number of frames for bullet
movement.
```

implementation

```
{$R *.lfm}

{ TForm1 }

// Initializes game settings and positions the star when the
form is created.
procedure TForm1.FormCreate(Sender: TObject);
begin
   Caption := 'Simple 2D Game with Math function with GPT4
by MoonWolf - Jan 26, 2024, Version 1.00';
   StarX := -ClientWidth div 2;
   CurrentFunctionIndex := 0;
   Timer1.Interval := TimerInterval;
   Timer1.Enabled := True;
   BulletActiveLeft := False;
   BulletActiveRight := False;
   Score := 0;
   ShowHitMessage := False;
   HitMessageTimer := 0;

   InitialMessageFontSize := 120; // Set initial font size for hit
message
   MaxHitMessageTimer := 15;        // Set maximum display
time for hit message
   FirstClickOccurred := False;    // Tracks if the first mouse
click has occurred
   FunctionRepeatCount := 0;
   GameOver := False;
end;

// Redraws the form including the grid, axes, functions, star,
bullets, and target mark.
procedure TForm1.FormPaint(Sender: TObject);
var
   CurrentFontSize: Integer;
   TextPosX, TextPosY: Integer;
begin
   Canvas.Brush.Color := clBlack;
   Canvas.FillRect(ClientRect);
   DrawGrid;
   DrawAxes;
   DrawFunctionText;

   StarY := CalculateY(StarX) + (ClientHeight div 2);
```

```pascal
    DrawStar(StarX + (ClientWidth div 2), StarY, StarSize,
StarColor, StarLineWidth);
    DrawStarCoordinates(StarX, StarY);

  if BulletActiveLeft then
    DrawBullet(BulletXLeft, BulletYLeft, BulletRadiusLeft);
  if BulletActiveRight then
    DrawBullet(BulletXRight, BulletYRight, BulletRadiusRight);
  if ShowTargetMark then
    DrawTargetMark(TargetX + TargetMarkAdjustX, TargetY +
TargetMarkAdjustY);
  DrawScore;

  if ShowHitMessage then
  begin
    CurrentFontSize := Max(12, InitialMessageFontSize *
HitMessageTimer div MaxHitMessageTimer);
    Canvas.Font.Size := CurrentFontSize;
    Canvas.Font.Color := clWhite;
    Canvas.TextOut(StarX + (ClientWidth div 2) -
CurrentFontSize * 2, StarY + 20, 'Nice Hit!');
  end;
end;

// Handles star and bullet movement, score updates, and game
over condition on each timer tick.
procedure TForm1.Timer1Timer(Sender: TObject);
var
  TextPosX, TextPosY: Integer;
begin
  // Independent movement of the star
  Inc(StarX, StarMoveStep);
  if StarX > ClientWidth div 2 then
  begin
    StarX := -ClientWidth div 2;
    Inc(CurrentFunctionIndex);
    if CurrentFunctionIndex >= Length(GraphFunctions) then
    begin
      CurrentFunctionIndex := 0;
      Inc(FunctionRepeatCount);
      if FunctionRepeatCount >= 2 then // Set condition for
Game Over
      begin
        GameOver := True;
        DisplayGameOverMessage; // Call new procedure to
display Game Over message
        Timer1.Enabled := False; // Stop the timer
        Exit; // Do not execute further code
```

164

```
        end;
      end;
    end
    else if StarX < -ClientWidth div 2 then
    begin
      StarX := ClientWidth div 2;
      CurrentFunctionIndex := (CurrentFunctionIndex + 1) mod
Length(GraphFunctions);
    end;

    // Adjusting the movement of the left bullet
    if BulletActiveLeft then
    begin
      BulletXLeft := BulletXLeft + DeltaXLeft;
      BulletYLeft := BulletYLeft + DeltaYLeft;
      BulletRadiusLeft := Max(BulletRadiusLeft - DeltaRadiusLeft,
10);

      if (Abs(BulletXLeft - TargetX) <= TargetHitTolerance) and
        (Abs(BulletYLeft - TargetY) <= TargetHitTolerance)
then
        begin
          BulletActiveLeft := False;
          BulletXLeft := TargetX;
          BulletYLeft := TargetY;
          BulletRadiusLeft := 10;
          if not BulletActiveRight then
            ShowTargetMark := False;
        end;
    end;

    // Adjusting the movement of the right bullet
    if BulletActiveRight then
    begin
      BulletXRight := BulletXRight + DeltaXRight;
      BulletYRight := BulletYRight + DeltaYRight;
      BulletRadiusRight := Max(BulletRadiusRight -
DeltaRadiusRight, 10);

      if (Abs(BulletXRight - TargetX) <= TargetHitTolerance) and
        (Abs(BulletYRight - TargetY) <= TargetHitTolerance)
then
        begin
          BulletActiveRight := False;
          BulletXRight := TargetX;
          BulletYRight := TargetY;
          BulletRadiusRight := 10;
          if not BulletActiveLeft then
```

```pascal
        ShowTargetMark := False;
    end;
  end;

  // Updating the score once the bullets have finished moving
  if (not BulletActiveLeft) and (not BulletActiveRight) and
FirstClickOccurred then
    begin
      // Hit detection
      if (Abs(StarX + (ClientWidth div 2) - TargetX) <=
HitTolerance) and
          (Abs(StarY - TargetY) <= HitTolerance) then
      begin
        Score := Score + ScoreHit;
        ShowHitMessage := True; // Display hit message
        HitMessageTimer := HitMessageDuration; // Set
message display duration
      end
      else
        Score := Score + ScoreMiss;

      // Reactivate bullets to prevent reactivation
      BulletActiveLeft := True;
      BulletActiveRight := True;
    end;

  if ShowHitMessage then
  begin
    Dec(HitMessageTimer);
    if HitMessageTimer <= 0 then
    begin
      ShowHitMessage := False;
    end;
  end;
  Invalidate; // Redrawing the screen
end;

// Initializes bullets and sets their trajectory when the mouse
button is pressed.
procedure TForm1.FormMouseDown(Sender: TObject;
Button: TMouseButton;
  Shift: TShiftState; X, Y: Integer);
const
  InitialBulletRadius = 100; // Initial radius of the bullets.
  FinalBulletRadius = 10;    // Final radius of the bullets.
  TotalFrames = 10;          // Number of frames for bullet
movement.
begin
```

```
    FirstClickOccurred := True; // Flag set to True when the
mouse is clicked

    TargetX := X; // Set the target X-coordinate to the clicked
position.
    TargetY := Y; // Set the target Y-coordinate to the clicked
position.

    // Initialize the left bullet at the left edge of the form.
    BulletActiveLeft := True;
    BulletXLeft := 0; // Start from the left edge.
    BulletYLeft := Form1.Height div 2; // Start from the vertical
center.
    BulletRadiusLeft := InitialBulletRadius; // Set the initial
radius.
    DeltaRadiusLeft := (InitialBulletRadius - FinalBulletRadius)
div TotalFrames; // Set radius decrease per frame.
    DeltaXLeft := (TargetX - BulletXLeft) div TotalFrames; // Set
horizontal movement per frame.
    DeltaYLeft := (TargetY - BulletYLeft) div TotalFrames; // Set
vertical movement per frame.

    // Initialize the right bullet at the right edge of the form.
    BulletActiveRight := True;
    BulletXRight := Form1.Width; // Start from the right edge.
    BulletYRight := Form1.Height div 2; // Start from the vertical
center.
    BulletRadiusRight := InitialBulletRadius; // Set the initial
radius.
    DeltaRadiusRight := (InitialBulletRadius - FinalBulletRadius)
div TotalFrames; // Set radius decrease per frame.
    DeltaXRight := (TargetX - BulletXRight) div TotalFrames; //
Set horizontal movement per frame.
    DeltaYRight := (TargetY - BulletYRight) div TotalFrames; //
Set vertical movement per frame.

    ShowTargetMark := True; // Show the target mark at the
clicked position.
end;

// Draws a star at the given position with specified size, color,
and line width.
procedure TForm1.DrawStar(const CenterX, CenterY,
Size: Integer;
                          const LineColor: TColor; const
LineWidth: Integer);
var
```

```
  Points: array[0..9] of TPoint; // Array to store the points of
the star.
  i: Integer;
  Angle: Double;
begin
  // Calculate the points of the star.
  for i := 0 to 4 do
  begin
    Angle := -Pi / 2 + (i * 2 * Pi / 5);
    Points[i * 2].X := CenterX + Round(Size * Cos(Angle));
    Points[i * 2].Y := CenterY + Round(Size * Sin(Angle));

    Angle := -Pi / 2 + ((i + 0.5) * 2 * Pi / 5);
    Points[i * 2 + 1].X := CenterX + Round(Size * Cos(Angle)
/ 2);
    Points[i * 2 + 1].Y := CenterY + Round(Size * Sin(Angle) /
2);
  end;

  // Draw the star by connecting the points.
  Canvas.Pen.Color := LineColor;
  Canvas.Pen.Width := LineWidth;
  Canvas.Brush.Style := bsClear;

  Canvas.MoveTo(Points[0].X, Points[0].Y);
  for i := 1 to 10 do
  begin
    Canvas.LineTo(Points[i mod 10].X, Points[i mod 10].Y);
  end;
end;

// Draws coordinate axes on the form.
procedure TForm1.DrawAxes;
begin
  // Drawing the X and Y axes in white.
  Canvas.Pen.Color := clWhite;
  Canvas.Pen.Width := 2;
  Canvas.MoveTo(0, ClientHeight div 2);
  Canvas.LineTo(ClientWidth, ClientHeight div 2);
  Canvas.MoveTo(ClientWidth div 2, 0);
  Canvas.LineTo(ClientWidth div 2, ClientHeight);

  // Labeling the axes.
  Canvas.Font.Color := AxisLabelFontColor;
  Canvas.Font.Size := AxisLabelFontSize;
  Canvas.TextOut(ClientWidth - 20, ClientHeight div 2 + 5,
'X');
  Canvas.TextOut(ClientWidth div 2 + 5, 5, 'Y');
```

```
    Canvas.TextOut(ClientWidth div 2 + 5, ClientHeight div 2 +
5, 'O');
end;

// Draws the grid on the form.
procedure TForm1.DrawGrid;
var
  i: Integer;
  GridX, GridY: Integer;
begin
  // Setting the grid color and line width.
  Canvas.Pen.Color := GridColor;
  Canvas.Pen.Width := 1;
  Canvas.Font.Size := GridLabelFontSize;

  // Drawing grid lines along the X-axis and labeling them.
  for i := -ClientWidth div 2 to ClientWidth div 2 do
  begin
    if (i mod GridSpacing = 0) and (i <> 0) then
    begin
      GridX := i + (ClientWidth div 2);
      Canvas.MoveTo(GridX, 0);
      Canvas.LineTo(GridX, ClientHeight);
      Canvas.TextOut(GridX - 10, ClientHeight div 2 + 5,
IntToStr(i));
    end;
  end;

  // Drawing grid lines along the Y-axis and labeling them.
  for i := -ClientHeight div 2 to ClientHeight div 2 do
  begin
    if (i mod GridSpacing = 0) and (i <> 0) then
    begin
      GridY := i + (ClientHeight div 2);
      Canvas.MoveTo(0, GridY);
      Canvas.LineTo(ClientWidth, GridY);
      Canvas.TextOut(ClientWidth div 2 + 5, GridY - 10,
IntToStr(-i));
    end;
  end;
end;

// Displays the current mathematical function as text on the
form.
procedure TForm1.DrawFunctionText;
begin
  // Setting the font color and size for the function text.
  Canvas.Font.Color := FunctionTextFontColor;
```

```pascal
  Canvas.Font.Size := FunctionTextFontSize;

  // Displaying the function text based on the current function
index.
  Canvas.TextOut(FunctionTextPositionX,
FunctionTextPositionY, FunctionTexts[CurrentFunctionIndex]);
end;

// Displays the coordinates of the star on the form.
procedure TForm1.DrawStarCoordinates(X, Y: Integer);
var
  CoordText: String;
begin
  // Formatting and displaying the star's coordinates.
  Y := -Y + (ClientHeight div 2); // Convert to Math Coordinate
Plane
  Canvas.Font.Color := StarCoordFontColor;
  Canvas.Font.Size := StarCoordFontSize;
  CoordText := Format('(X=%d, Y=%d)', [X, Y]);
  Canvas.TextOut(StarCoordPositionX, StarCoordPositionY,
CoordText);
end;

// Draws a bullet at the specified position with the given radius.
procedure TForm1.DrawBullet(const X, Y, Radius:
Integer);
begin
  // Setting the color and border width for the bullet.
  Canvas.Pen.Color := BulletColor;
  Canvas.Pen.Width := BulletBorderWidth;
  Canvas.Brush.Style := bsClear;

  // Drawing the bullet as an ellipse.
  Canvas.Ellipse(X - Radius, Y - Radius, X + Radius, Y +
Radius);
end;

// Displays the current score on the form.
procedure TForm1.DrawScore;
begin
  // Setting the font color and size for the score.
  Canvas.Font.Color := clWhite;
  Canvas.Font.Size := 20;

  // Displaying the score text.
  Canvas.TextOut(10, 10, 'Score: ' + IntToStr(Score));
end;
```

```
// Draws a target mark at the specified position.
procedure TForm1.DrawTargetMark(const X, Y: Integer);
begin
  // Setting the color for the target mark.
  Canvas.Pen.Color := TargetMarkColor;

  // Drawing horizontal and vertical lines to represent the
target mark.
  Canvas.MoveTo(X - TargetMarkSize, Y);
  Canvas.LineTo(X + TargetMarkSize, Y);
  Canvas.MoveTo(X, Y - TargetMarkSize);
  Canvas.LineTo(X, Y + TargetMarkSize);
end;

// Calculates the Y-coordinate for the current function based on
the given X-coordinate.
function TForm1.CalculateY(X: Integer): Integer;
begin

  // Calculating the Y-coordinate based on the selected function.

  case GraphFunctions[CurrentFunctionIndex] of

      0: Result := Round(0.0077 * Power(X, 2)-150);
      1: Result := Round(Abs(0.5 * X +100 ));
      2: Result := Round(150 * Sin(0.03 * X));
      3: if X <> 0 then
           //Result := Round(7000 / X)
           Result := Round(9000 / X)
         else
           Result := 0;
      4: if Cos(0.0099 * X) <> 0 then
           Result := Round(10*Sin(0.0099 * X) / Cos(0.0099
* X))
         else
           Result := 0;
    else
      Result := 0;
    end;

    Result := - Result; // From1's Y direction is downward

end;


procedure TForm1.FormKeyDown(Sender: TObject; var
Key: Word; Shift: TShiftState);
```

```
begin
  // Reset game if space key is pressed after Game Over
  if (Key = VK_SPACE) and GameOver then
  begin
    Score := 0;
    FunctionRepeatCount := 0;
    GameOver := False;
    Timer1.Enabled := True;
  end;

  // Shortcut for moving the star to a specific position
  // This is hidden command to reduce star moving time
  if (Key = VK_Right) then
  begin
    StarX := 300;
  end;

end;

{
procedure TForm1.ShowGameOverMessage; // This is only for
debug
begin
  ShowMessage('Game Over');
end;
}

// Displays the game over message.
procedure TForm1.DisplayGameOverMessage;
begin
  // Setting font properties for Game Over message
  Canvas.Font.Size := 30;
  Canvas.Font.Color := clyellow;

  // Displaying Game Over message and score, centered on
the screen
  Canvas.TextOut((ClientWidth - Canvas.TextWidth('Game
Over')) div 2, (ClientHeight div 2) - 50, 'Game Over');
  Canvas.TextOut((ClientWidth - Canvas.TextWidth('Your
Score = ' + IntToStr(Score))) div 2, ClientHeight div 2, 'Your
Score = ' + IntToStr(Score));
  Canvas.TextOut((ClientWidth - Canvas.TextWidth('Hit Space
Key to replay')) div 2, (ClientHeight div 2) + 50, 'Hit Space Key
to replay');
end;

end.
```

This is pure program without comment. The program written in Pascal is already easy to read. Some people will need this simple version.

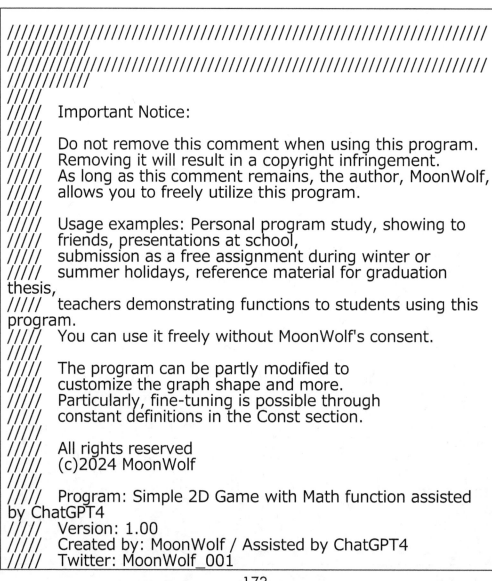

```
/////////////////////////////////////////////////////////////////////
///////////
/////////////////////////////////////////////////////////////////////
///////////
/////
/////    Important Notice:
/////
/////    Do not remove this comment when using this program.
/////    Removing it will result in a copyright infringement.
/////    As long as this comment remains, the author, MoonWolf,
/////    allows you to freely utilize this program.
/////
/////    Usage examples: Personal program study, showing to
/////    friends, presentations at school,
/////    submission as a free assignment during winter or
/////    summer holidays, reference material for graduation
thesis,
/////    teachers demonstrating functions to students using this
program.
/////    You can use it freely without MoonWolf's consent.
/////
/////    The program can be partly modified to
/////    customize the graph shape and more.
/////    Particularly, fine-tuning is possible through
/////    constant definitions in the Const section.
/////
/////    All rights reserved
/////    (c)2024 MoonWolf
/////
/////    Program: Simple 2D Game with Math function assisted
by ChatGPT4
/////    Version: 1.00
/////    Created by: MoonWolf / Assisted by ChatGPT4
/////    Twitter: MoonWolf_001
```

```
/////   Development Environment: Window11 + Lazarus 2.2.6
/////   Release Date: January 26, 2024
/////
/////   Remarks:
/////
/////   Lazarus is a programming development environment.
/////   It's a free programming development environment.
/////   The programming language is Pascal.
/////   For programming beginners, it's less difficult than
/////   C language-based ones and easy to get started.
/////   Pascal is used as an educational programming language
in the world.
/////   Lazarus is simple and powerful.
/////   Almost all Windows apps can be developed using
Lazarus.
/////
/////   Lazarus Official Website:
/////   https://lazarus-ide.org
/////
/////   Reference Book:
/////
/////   SIMPLE 2D GAME: PASCAL Programming
/////
/////   Author MoonWolf JP. Published in 2023
/////   Available as Kindle e-books and paperback.
/////   Also available for unlimited reading for Kindle Unlimited
subscribers.
/////   Amazon Link:
/////   https://www.amazon.com/dp/B0CHN7PK88
/////
/////   Disclaimer:
/////   MoonWolf does not provide support for Windows
knowledge,
/////   Lazarus installation,
/////   questions about Lazarus, errors that occur,
/////   and any other issues or questions related to these.
/////   Please research and solve these issues on your own.
/////   Using the free version of ChatPGT3.5
/////   can potentially help solve these efficiently.
/////   Using the paid version of ChatGPT4
/////   can potentially help solve these more efficiently.
/////
/////////////////////////////////////////////////////////////////
/////////////
/////////////////////////////////////////////////////////////////
/////////////

unit Unit1;
```

```
{$mode objfpc}{$H+}

interface

uses
  Classes, SysUtils, Forms, Controls, Graphics, ExtCtrls, Math,
LCLType, Dialogs;

type
  TForm1 = class(TForm)
    Timer1: TTimer;
    procedure FormCreate(Sender: TObject);
    procedure FormKeyDown(Sender: TObject; var Key: Word;
Shift: TShiftState);
    procedure FormPaint(Sender: TObject);
    procedure Timer1Timer(Sender: TObject);
    procedure FormMouseDown(Sender: TObject; Button:
TMouseButton;
       Shift: TShiftState; X, Y: Integer);
  private
    ShowHitMessage: Boolean;
    HitMessageTimer: Integer;
    FunctionRepeatCount: Integer;
    GameOver: Boolean;
    StarX, StarY: Integer;
    CurrentFunctionIndex: Integer;
    BulletActiveLeft, BulletActiveRight: Boolean;
    BulletXLeft, BulletYLeft: Integer;
    BulletXRight, BulletYRight: Integer;
    TargetX, TargetY: Integer;
    Score: Integer;
    ShowTargetMark: Boolean;
    BulletRadiusLeft, BulletRadiusRight: Integer;
    DeltaXLeft, DeltaYLeft: Integer;
    DeltaXRight, DeltaYRight: Integer;
    DeltaRadiusLeft, DeltaRadiusRight: Integer;
    InitialMessageFontSize: Integer;
    MaxHitMessageTimer: Integer;
    FirstClickOccurred: Boolean;
    procedure DisplayGameOverMessage;
    procedure DrawStar(const CenterX, CenterY, Size: Integer;
                       const LineColor: TColor; const
LineWidth: Integer);
    procedure DrawAxes;
    procedure DrawGrid;
    procedure DrawFunctionText;
    procedure DrawStarCoordinates(X, Y: Integer);
```

```
      procedure DrawBullet(const X, Y, Radius: Integer);
      procedure DrawScore;
      procedure DrawTargetMark(const X, Y: Integer);
      function CalculateY(X: Integer): Integer;
    public
    end;

var
  Form1: TForm1;

const
  StarSize = 20;
  StarColor = clYellow;
  StarLineWidth = 7;
  GraphScale = 100;
  GraphFunctions: array[0..4] of Integer = (0, 1, 2, 3, 4);
  FunctionTexts: array[0..4] of string = (
    'Y = 0.0077 * X^2 - 150',
    'Y = |0.5 * X + 100|',
    'Y = 150 * Sin(0.03 * X)',
    'Y = 9000 / X (X ≠ 0)',
    'Y = 10 * tan(0.0099 * X) (cos(0.0099X) ≠ 0)'
  );
  FunctionTextFontColor = clWhite;
  FunctionTextFontSize = 25;
  FunctionTextPositionX = 10;
  FunctionTextPositionY = 400;
  AxisLabelFontColor = clWhite;
  AxisLabelFontSize = 8;
  ArrowSize = 10;
  GridColor = clGray;
  GridSpacing = 50;
  GridLabelFontSize = 8;
  TimerInterval = 40;
  StarMoveStep = 5;
  StarCoordFontColor = clWhite;
  StarCoordFontSize = 25;
  StarCoordPositionX = 10;
  StarCoordPositionY = 450;
  HitMessageDuration = 14;
  InitialBulletRadius = 50;
  FinalBulletRadius = 10;
  BulletShrinkRate = 5;
  BulletSpeed = 5;
  HitTolerance = 15;
  ScoreHit = 100;
  ScoreMiss = -10;
  BulletColor = clRed;
```

```pascal
    BulletBorderWidth = 5;
    TargetHitTolerance = 15;
    TargetMarkColor = clLime;
    TargetMarkSize = 10;
    TargetMarkAdjustX = 0;
    TargetMarkAdjustY = 0;
    TotalFrames = 20;

implementation

{$R *.lfm}

procedure TForm1.FormCreate(Sender: TObject);
begin
    Caption := 'Simple 2D Game with Math function with GPT4
by MoonWolf - Jan 26, 2024, Version 1.00';
    StarX := -ClientWidth div 2;
    CurrentFunctionIndex := 0;
    Timer1.Interval := TimerInterval;
    Timer1.Enabled := True;
    BulletActiveLeft := False;
    BulletActiveRight := False;
    Score := 0;
    ShowHitMessage := False;
    HitMessageTimer := 0;
    InitialMessageFontSize := 120;
    MaxHitMessageTimer := 15;
    FirstClickOccurred := False;
    FunctionRepeatCount := 0;
    GameOver := False;
end;

procedure TForm1.FormPaint(Sender: TObject);
var
    CurrentFontSize: Integer;
    TextPosX, TextPosY: Integer;
begin
    Canvas.Brush.Color := clBlack;
    Canvas.FillRect(ClientRect);
    DrawGrid;
    DrawAxes;
    DrawFunctionText;
    StarY := CalculateY(StarX) + (ClientHeight div 2);
    DrawStar(StarX + (ClientWidth div 2), StarY, StarSize,
StarColor, StarLineWidth);
    DrawStarCoordinates(StarX, StarY);
    if BulletActiveLeft then
        DrawBullet(BulletXLeft, BulletYLeft, BulletRadiusLeft);
```

```
  if BulletActiveRight then
    DrawBullet(BulletXRight, BulletYRight, BulletRadiusRight);
  if ShowTargetMark then
    DrawTargetMark(TargetX + TargetMarkAdjustX, TargetY +
TargetMarkAdjustY);
  DrawScore;
  if ShowHitMessage then
  begin
    CurrentFontSize := Max(12, InitialMessageFontSize *
HitMessageTimer div MaxHitMessageTimer);
    Canvas.Font.Size := CurrentFontSize;
    Canvas.Font.Color := clWhite;
    Canvas.TextOut(StarX + (ClientWidth div 2) -
CurrentFontSize * 2, StarY + 20, 'Nice Hit!');
  end;
end;

procedure TForm1.Timer1Timer(Sender: TObject);
var
  TextPosX, TextPosY: Integer;
begin
  Inc(StarX, StarMoveStep);
  if StarX > ClientWidth div 2 then
  begin
    StarX := -ClientWidth div 2;
    Inc(CurrentFunctionIndex);
    if CurrentFunctionIndex >= Length(GraphFunctions) then
    begin
      CurrentFunctionIndex := 0;
      Inc(FunctionRepeatCount);
      if FunctionRepeatCount >= 2 then
      begin
        GameOver := True;
        DisplayGameOverMessage;
        Timer1.Enabled := False;
        Exit;
      end;
    end;
  end
  else if StarX < -ClientWidth div 2 then
  begin
    StarX := ClientWidth div 2;
    CurrentFunctionIndex := (CurrentFunctionIndex + 1) mod
Length(GraphFunctions);
  end;
  if BulletActiveLeft then
  begin
    BulletXLeft := BulletXLeft + DeltaXLeft;
```

```pascal
    BulletYLeft := BulletYLeft + DeltaYLeft;
    BulletRadiusLeft := Max(BulletRadiusLeft - DeltaRadiusLeft,
10);
      if (Abs(BulletXLeft - TargetX) <= TargetHitTolerance) and
         (Abs(BulletYLeft - TargetY) <= TargetHitTolerance)
then
      begin
        BulletActiveLeft := False;
        BulletXLeft := TargetX;
        BulletYLeft := TargetY;
        BulletRadiusLeft := 10;
        if not BulletActiveRight then
           ShowTargetMark := False;
      end;
    end;
    if BulletActiveRight then
    begin
      BulletXRight := BulletXRight + DeltaXRight;
      BulletYRight := BulletYRight + DeltaYRight;
      BulletRadiusRight := Max(BulletRadiusRight -
DeltaRadiusRight, 10);
      if (Abs(BulletXRight - TargetX) <= TargetHitTolerance) and
         (Abs(BulletYRight - TargetY) <= TargetHitTolerance)
then
      begin
        BulletActiveRight := False;
        BulletXRight := TargetX;
        BulletYRight := TargetY;
        BulletRadiusRight := 10;
        if not BulletActiveLeft then
           ShowTargetMark := False;
      end;
    end;
    if (not BulletActiveLeft) and (not BulletActiveRight) and
FirstClickOccurred then
    begin
      if (Abs(StarX + (ClientWidth div 2) - TargetX) <=
HitTolerance) and
         (Abs(StarY - TargetY) <= HitTolerance) then
      begin
        Score := Score + ScoreHit;
        ShowHitMessage := True;
        HitMessageTimer := HitMessageDuration;
      end
      else
        Score := Score + ScoreMiss;
      BulletActiveLeft := True;
      BulletActiveRight := True;
```

```pascal
      end;
    if ShowHitMessage then
    begin
      Dec(HitMessageTimer);
      if HitMessageTimer <= 0 then
      begin
        ShowHitMessage := False;
      end;
    end;
    Invalidate;
end;

procedure TForm1.FormMouseDown(Sender: TObject; Button:
TMouseButton;
    Shift: TShiftState; X, Y: Integer);
const
    InitialBulletRadius = 100;
    FinalBulletRadius = 10;
    TotalFrames = 10;
begin
    FirstClickOccurred := True;
    TargetX := X;
    TargetY := Y;
    BulletActiveLeft := True;
    BulletXLeft := 0;
    BulletYLeft := Form1.Height div 2;
    BulletRadiusLeft := InitialBulletRadius;
    DeltaRadiusLeft := (InitialBulletRadius - FinalBulletRadius)
div TotalFrames;
    DeltaXLeft := (TargetX - BulletXLeft) div TotalFrames;
    DeltaYLeft := (TargetY - BulletYLeft) div TotalFrames;
    BulletActiveRight := True;
    BulletXRight := Form1.Width;
    BulletYRight := Form1.Height div 2;
    BulletRadiusRight := InitialBulletRadius;
    DeltaRadiusRight := (InitialBulletRadius - FinalBulletRadius)
div TotalFrames;
    DeltaXRight := (TargetX - BulletXRight) div TotalFrames;
    DeltaYRight := (TargetY - BulletYRight) div TotalFrames;
    ShowTargetMark := True;
end;


procedure TForm1.DrawStar(const CenterX, CenterY, Size:
Integer;
                          const LineColor: TColor; const
LineWidth: Integer);
var
```

```
    Points: array[0..9] of TPoint;
    i: Integer;
    Angle: Double;
begin
  for i := 0 to 4 do
  begin
     Angle := -Pi / 2 + (i * 2 * Pi / 5);
     Points[i * 2].X := CenterX + Round(Size * Cos(Angle));
     Points[i * 2].Y := CenterY + Round(Size * Sin(Angle));

     Angle := -Pi / 2 + ((i + 0.5) * 2 * Pi / 5);
     Points[i * 2 + 1].X := CenterX + Round(Size * Cos(Angle)
/ 2);
     Points[i * 2 + 1].Y := CenterY + Round(Size * Sin(Angle) /
2);
  end;

  Canvas.Pen.Color := LineColor;
  Canvas.Pen.Width := LineWidth;
  Canvas.Brush.Style := bsClear;

  Canvas.MoveTo(Points[0].X, Points[0].Y);
  for i := 1 to 10 do
  begin
     Canvas.LineTo(Points[i mod 10].X, Points[i mod 10].Y);
  end;
end;

procedure TForm1.DrawAxes;
begin
  Canvas.Pen.Color := clWhite;
  Canvas.Pen.Width := 2;
  Canvas.MoveTo(0, ClientHeight div 2);
  Canvas.LineTo(ClientWidth, ClientHeight div 2);
  Canvas.MoveTo(ClientWidth div 2, 0);
  Canvas.LineTo(ClientWidth div 2, ClientHeight);

  Canvas.Font.Color := AxisLabelFontColor;
  Canvas.Font.Size := AxisLabelFontSize;
  Canvas.TextOut(ClientWidth - 20, ClientHeight div 2 + 5,
'X');
  Canvas.TextOut(ClientWidth div 2 + 5, 5, 'Y');
  Canvas.TextOut(ClientWidth div 2 + 5, ClientHeight div 2 +
5, 'O');
end;

procedure TForm1.DrawGrid;
var
```

```
  i: Integer;
  GridX, GridY: Integer;
begin
  Canvas.Pen.Color := GridColor;
  Canvas.Pen.Width := 1;
  Canvas.Font.Size := GridLabelFontSize;

  for i := -ClientWidth div 2 to ClientWidth div 2 do
  begin
    if (i mod GridSpacing = 0) and (i <> 0) then
    begin
      GridX := i + (ClientWidth div 2);
      Canvas.MoveTo(GridX, 0);
      Canvas.LineTo(GridX, ClientHeight);
      Canvas.TextOut(GridX - 10, ClientHeight div 2 + 5,
IntToStr(i));
    end;
  end;

  for i := -ClientHeight div 2 to ClientHeight div 2 do
  begin
    if (i mod GridSpacing = 0) and (i <> 0) then
    begin
      GridY := i + (ClientHeight div 2);
      Canvas.MoveTo(0, GridY);
      Canvas.LineTo(ClientWidth, GridY);
      Canvas.TextOut(ClientWidth div 2 + 5, GridY - 10,
IntToStr(-i));
    end;
  end;
end;

procedure TForm1.DrawFunctionText;
begin
  Canvas.Font.Color := FunctionTextFontColor;
  Canvas.Font.Size := FunctionTextFontSize;
  Canvas.TextOut(FunctionTextPositionX,
FunctionTextPositionY, FunctionTexts[CurrentFunctionIndex]);
end;

procedure TForm1.DrawStarCoordinates(X, Y: Integer);
var
  CoordText: String;
begin
  Y := -Y + (ClientHeight div 2);
  Canvas.Font.Color := StarCoordFontColor;
  Canvas.Font.Size := StarCoordFontSize;
  CoordText := Format('(X=%d, Y=%d)', [X, Y]);
```

```
    Canvas.TextOut(StarCoordPositionX, StarCoordPositionY,
CoordText);
end;

procedure TForm1.DrawBullet(const X, Y, Radius: Integer);
begin
  Canvas.Pen.Color := BulletColor;
  Canvas.Pen.Width := BulletBorderWidth;
  Canvas.Brush.Style := bsClear;
  Canvas.Ellipse(X - Radius, Y - Radius, X + Radius, Y +
Radius);
end;

procedure TForm1.DrawScore;
begin
  Canvas.Font.Color := clWhite;
  Canvas.Font.Size := 20;
  Canvas.TextOut(10, 10, 'Score: ' + IntToStr(Score));
end;

procedure TForm1.DrawTargetMark(const X, Y: Integer);
begin
  Canvas.Pen.Color := TargetMarkColor;
  Canvas.MoveTo(X - TargetMarkSize, Y);
  Canvas.LineTo(X + TargetMarkSize, Y);
  Canvas.MoveTo(X, Y - TargetMarkSize);
  Canvas.LineTo(X, Y + TargetMarkSize);
end;

function TForm1.CalculateY(X: Integer): Integer;
begin
  case GraphFunctions[CurrentFunctionIndex] of
    0: Result := Round(0.0077 * Power(X, 2)-150);
    1: Result := Round(Abs(0.5 * X +100 ));
    2: Result := Round(150 * Sin(0.03 * X));
    3: if X <> 0 then
         Result := Round(9000 / X)
       else
         Result := 0;
    4: if Cos(0.0099 * X) <> 0 then
         Result := Round(10*Sin(0.0099 * X) / Cos(0.0099 *
X))
       else
         Result := 0;
  else
    Result := 0;
  end;
  Result := - Result;
```

```
end;

procedure TForm1.FormKeyDown(Sender: TObject; var Key:
Word; Shift: TShiftState);
begin
  if (Key = VK_SPACE) and GameOver then
  begin
    Score := 0;
    FunctionRepeatCount := 0;
    GameOver := False;
    Timer1.Enabled := True;
  end;
  if (Key = VK_Right) then
  begin
    StarX := 300;
  end;
end;

procedure TForm1.DisplayGameOverMessage;
begin
  Canvas.Font.Size := 30;
  Canvas.Font.Color := clyellow;
  Canvas.TextOut((ClientWidth - Canvas.TextWidth('Game
Over')) div 2, (ClientHeight div 2) - 50, 'Game Over');
  Canvas.TextOut((ClientWidth - Canvas.TextWidth('Your
Score = ' + IntToStr(Score))) div 2, ClientHeight div 2, 'Your
Score = ' + IntToStr(Score));
  Canvas.TextOut((ClientWidth - Canvas.TextWidth('Hit Space
Key to replay')) div 2, (ClientHeight div 2) + 50, 'Hit Space Key
to replay');
end;

end.
```

This game is a simple yet engaging 2D game that utilizes Form1, Timer1, and Canvas in Lazarus, programmed in Pascal.

The game cleverly integrates mathematical functions with interactive gameplay, offering both entertainment and educational value.

Game Description

Title: Simple 2D Game with Mathematical Functions

Platform: Developed in Lazarus using Pascal

Key Features:

Graphical Display:

The game uses the Canvas to render a coordinate plane, display the movement of a star, visualize bullet effects, and show real-time updates.

Star Movement:

A star moves across the screen from left to right, following predefined mathematical functions.
Player Interaction: The player's primary action is to click the mouse to aim at the moving star.

Targeting Mechanism:

Upon clicking, a '+' mark appears at the clicked coordinates. Bullets are then shot towards this mark from both sides of the screen, taking about 0.5 seconds to reach.

Gameplay Strategy:

The challenge lies in anticipating the star's movement rather than clicking directly on it. This introduces an element of skill and prediction, creating a finely balanced gameplay experience.

Scoring System:

The game's score is determined by how accurately the player can hit the star as it cycles through the mathematical functions twice. Points are awarded for hitting the star and deducted for missing it.

Educational Aspect:

Beyond just being a game, it sparks interest in mathematical functions and graphs, potentially making math feel more approachable and relevant.

Conclusion

This game is not just a source of fun but also serves as an educational tool, making mathematical concepts more tangible and engaging. It's a unique blend of gaming and learning, ideal for anyone interested in experiencing math in a new and interactive way. Give it a try and enjoy the blend of mathematics and gaming!

Uses Clause

The uses section includes essential modules like Classes, SysUtils, Forms, Controls, Graphics, ExtCtrls, Math, LCLType, and Dialogs. These modules provide foundational functionalities for the game, such as form controls, graphical elements, mathematical operations, and system utilities.

Form1 Content

TForm1 is the main form class for the application. It's responsible for handling visual elements and game logic. Key components include:

Timer1:

A timer for continuous updates during gameplay.
Event procedures for form creation (FormCreate), key presses (FormKeyDown), painting (FormPaint), timer ticks (Timer1Timer), and mouse clicks (FormMouseDown).

Private Declarations

The private section of TForm1 contains variables and procedures that manage the game's internal state and mechanics. This includes:

Variables for tracking the star's position, bullet states, scoring, and game over conditions.
Procedures for drawing game elements like the star, bullets, and grid, and for calculating the star's position based on mathematical functions.

187

Constant Declarations

The const section defines constants for graphical elements and game mechanics. These constants allow for easy adjustments and fine-tuning of the game's appearance and behavior. This includes settings for the star's size and color, mathematical functions, bullet mechanics, and UI elements like font sizes and colors.

Procedures Overview

FormCreate (Sender: TObject):

Initializes the game when the form is created.
Sets up initial game settings, such as the starting position of the star, initial function index, and game state variables.

FormPaint (Sender: TObject):

Responsible for drawing all the visual elements on the form whenever it needs to be repainted.
This includes the star, bullets, grid, axes, function text, star coordinates, and target mark.

Timer1Timer (Sender: TObject):

Triggered on each timer tick, it handles the game's main loop.
Manages the movement of the star and bullets, updates scores, and checks for game over conditions.

FormMouseDown (Sender: TObject; Button: TMouseButton; Shift: TShiftState; X, Y: Integer):

Activates when the mouse button is clicked.
Sets the target coordinates for the bullets and initializes their movement towards the clicked position.

DrawStar (const CenterX, CenterY, Size: Integer; const LineColor: TColor; const LineWidth: Integer):

Draws a star at a specified position with a given size, color, and line width.

DrawAxes:

Renders the coordinate axes on the form.

DrawGrid:

Draws a grid on the form, aiding in visualizing the coordinate plane.

DrawFunctionText:

Displays the current mathematical function as text on the form.

DrawStarCoordinates (X, Y: Integer):

Shows the current coordinates of the star.

DrawBullet (const X, Y, Radius: Integer):

Draws a bullet at a specified position with a given radius.

DrawScore:

Displays the current score on the form.

DrawTargetMark (const X, Y: Integer):

Draws a target mark at the specified position.

CalculateY (X: Integer): Integer:

Calculates the Y-coordinate for the star based on the current mathematical function.

FormKeyDown (Sender: TObject; var Key: Word; Shift: TShiftState):

Handles keyboard inputs.
Includes functionality for restarting the game and other key-based controls.

DisplayGameOverMessage:

Displays a game over message along with the final score.

Setting Up in Lazarus

[1] Copy and Paste the Program Code:

Open Lazarus and navigate to the code editor.
Copy the provided Pascal source code.
Paste it into the Lazarus code editor, overwriting any existing code.

[2] Configuring the Object Inspector in Lazarus

a. FormCreate (Linking to OnCreate Event)

Select Form1 in the Object Inspector.
Click on the "Events" tab in the middle of the Object Inspector.
Find the OnCreate event in the list of events.
Click the "..." button next to the OnCreate event. This links the FormCreate procedure in your code to the OnCreate event of Form1.

b. FormKeyDown (Linking to OnKeyDown Event)

Ensure Form1 is still selected in the Object Inspector.
Locate the OnKeyDown event in the Events tab.
Click the "..." button next to OnKeyDown. This action links the FormKeyDown procedure to the OnKeyDown event of Form1.

c. FormPaint (Linking to OnPaint Event)

With Form1 selected, go to the Events tab in the Object Inspector.
Find the OnPaint event in the list.
Click the "..." button next to OnPaint. This links the FormPaint procedure to the OnPaint event of Form1.

d. Timer1Timer (Linking to OnTimer Event)

Add Timer1 to your form if it's not already there, and select it in the Object Inspector.
Navigate to the OnTimer event in the Events tab.
Click the "..." button next to OnTimer. This links the Timer1Timer procedure to the OnTimer event of Timer1.

e. FormMouseDown (Linking to OnMouseDown Event)

Select Form1 again in the Object Inspector.
In the Events tab, locate the OnMouseDown event.
Click the "..." button next to OnMouseDown. This links the FormMouseDown procedure to the OnMouseDown event of Form1.

[3] Compile the Program:

After setting up the Object Inspector, compile the program to check for any syntactical errors.
Use the "Compile" or "Run" option in Lazarus to build the project.

[4] Run the Program:

Once the compilation is successful without errors, run the program.
Check for any runtime issues or bugs during the execution of the game.

[1] Star Movement and Program Logic

Overview of Star Movement

The star in the game moves from the left to the right side of the screen. Its horizontal movement (StarX) is linear and constant. The vertical position (StarY) of the star is dynamically calculated based on various mathematical functions, changing as StarX increases.

Connection Between Function Texts and Program

Implementation

The game displays mathematical functions as text, and these functions are directly used in the program to calculate the star's vertical position. The specific functions are:

Quadratic Function:

Displayed as 'Y = 0.0077 * X^2 - 150'.

In the program: Result := Round(0.0077 * Power(X, 2) - 150); This creates a parabolic trajectory for the star.

Absolute Value Function:

Displayed as 'Y = |0.5 * X + 100|'.

In the program: Result := Round(Abs(0.5 * X + 100));
The star follows a V-shaped path.

Sine Function:

Displayed as 'Y = 150 * Sin(0.03 * X)'.

In the program: Result := Round(150 * Sin(0.03 * X));
The star moves in a sinusoidal, wave-like pattern.

Inverse Function:

Displayed as 'Y = 9000 / X (X ≠ 0)'.

In the program: if X <> 0 then Result := Round(9000 / X) else
Result := 0;
Ensures that division by zero is avoided, creating a hyperbolic
movement.

Tangent Function:

Displayed as 'Y = 10 * tan(0.0099 * X) (cos(0.0099X) ≠ 0)'.

In the program: if Cos(0.0099 * X) <> 0 then Result :=
Round(10 * Sin(0.0099 * X) / Cos(0.0099 * X)) else Result := 0;
Prevents undefined values, resulting in a sharp, periodic change
in the star's path.

Implementation Details

X in the program is the actual value of the star's horizontal
position, used directly in the mathematical functions.

The CalculateY function is called within the Timer1Timer procedure, which is the main game loop. This loop updates the star's position at regular intervals.

As StarX increases with each timer tick, CalculateY recalculates StarY based on the current function, resulting in the star tracing the graph of that function across the screen.

The negative sign (-) in the final assignment to Result aligns the mathematical functions with the screen's coordinate system, where the Y-axis is positive downwards.

[2] Hit Detection and Subsequent Processing

Core Variables for Hit Detection

BulletXLeft, BulletYLeft, BulletXRight, BulletYRight: These variables represent the coordinates of the bullets shot from the left and right sides of the screen.

TargetX, TargetY: Coordinates where the mouse was clicked, serving as the target for the bullets.

StarX, StarY: Current coordinates of the star.

HitTolerance: A predefined constant that specifies the allowable margin for a hit to be considered successful.
Hit Detection Logic

Bullet Movement and Targeting:

When the player clicks the mouse, FormMouseDown is triggered, setting TargetX and TargetY to the mouse click coordinates.

Bullets are then "fired" towards these coordinates, with their positions (BulletXLeft, BulletYLeft, BulletXRight, BulletYRight) updated in the Timer1Timer procedure.

Checking for Hits:

The crucial part of hit detection occurs in the Timer1Timer procedure.

The game checks if the bullets have reached the vicinity of the star. This is done by comparing the bullet coordinates with the star's coordinates (StarX, StarY), considering the HitTolerance.

A hit is registered if the distance between the bullets and the star is less than or equal to HitTolerance.

Processing After a Hit

Score Update:

If a hit is detected, the player's score is updated. This is managed by the Score variable.
Points are added for a successful hit and deducted for a miss.

Visual Feedback on Hit

"Nice Hit!" Message Display:

Upon a successful hit, a "Nice Hit!" message is displayed on the screen.

This feature is managed by two variables: ShowHitMessage (a boolean flag) and HitMessageTimer (an integer for timing the display duration).

Hit Message Animation:

The animation effect of the Hit message moving towards the star is achieved by dynamically changing its position and size over time.

In the FormPaint procedure, the position and font size of the "Nice Hit!" message are adjusted based on HitMessageTimer.

The message starts large and gradually decreases in size, giving the impression of moving towards the star's position.

Timing and Positioning:

The Timer1Timer procedure decrements HitMessageTimer, controlling how long the message is displayed and its movement speed.

The message's initial position is set relative to where the hit occurred, and it moves closer to the star's position as HitMessageTimer decreases.

After a hit or miss, the bullets are reset for the next shot, and the target mark is removed or repositioned based on the next mouse click.

Introduction

I began my journey in game programming at the age of 13, using a language called BASIC. That was over 40 years ago. My initial foray into this world was with the SEGA-SC3000 gaming console, creating games using a BASIC cartridge.

Data was stored on cassette tapes, recorded in audio format. I eagerly awaited monthly gaming magazines, and each month, I would input the code from these magazines into my console.

At that time, I didn't fully understand the meaning behind the code, but I was fascinated by the ability to bring games to life through my own efforts.

There was no one around to teach me about programming, and I was the only one in my school year who could write code.

Starting from scratch to create a game is a challenging task. One of the first things I did was to tweak variables and other aspects of games created by others.

This allowed me to gain a deeper understanding of the games I assembled. I would make small modifications to the game code, and these incremental steps were the starting point of my journey in game creation.

In this chapter, I want to guide you through modifying and adding to the program I have created. By making these changes, you can gain a deeper understanding and enjoyment of the content in this book.

In creating this program, I have gathered parameters in the Const section at the beginning to allow for easy adjustment of the game balance.

I recommend that you start by experimenting with these constants to see how slight changes can alter the gameplay. Here's how modifying each of these variables can impact the game:

StarSize = 20;

This constant determines the size of the star. Increasing the value will make the star larger, potentially making it easier to hit. Conversely, decreasing this value will make the star smaller and more challenging to target.

StarColor = clYellow;

This constant sets the color of the star. Changing this value will alter the star's appearance, which can affect visual clarity and player experience. Different colors might make the star more or less visible against the game's background.

TimerInterval = 40;

This constant controls the interval (in milliseconds) at which the game's main loop (Timer1Timer) is executed. Decreasing this value will speed up the game, making the star and bullets move faster. Increasing it will slow down the game, which might make it easier for beginners.

InitialBulletRadius = 50;

This constant defines the initial radius of the bullets. A larger radius makes the bullets appear bigger when they are first shot, which could affect the game's visual style and the player's perception of the bullet's trajectory.

BulletColor = clRed;

Similar to StarColor, this constant sets the color of the bullets. Changing the color can impact how easily the bullets are seen and can be used to increase or decrease the game's visual complexity.

TargetMarkSize = 10;

This constant determines the size of the target mark that appears when the player clicks the mouse. A larger size makes the target mark more visible, which might help players in aiming. A smaller size could increase the challenge.

TotalFrames = 20;

This constant affects the number of frames over which the bullets move towards the target. Increasing this number will make the bullets move slower and more gradually, while decreasing it will make the bullets reach the target faster.

Typical Color list of Lazarus

clRed:

Represents the color red. Use this to make the star appear red.

clBlue:

Represents the color blue. This can be used for a blue star.

clGreen:

Represents the color green. Choose this for a green star.

clWhite:

Represents the color white. This makes the star white, which might be useful for contrast against a darker background.

clBlack:

Represents the color black. A black star can be striking against a lighter background.

clGray:

Represents the color gray. This is a neutral color that can give the star a subdued appearance.

clPurple:

Represents the color purple. This can be used for a more unusual or vibrant star color.

clFuchsia:

Represents a bright pink-purple color, similar to fuchsia. It's a vivid choice for the star.

clAqua:

Represents a cyan or aqua color. This gives the star a bright, water-like hue.

clLime:

Represents a bright, lime green color. It's a more vivid alternative to clGreen.

In this section, we'll delve into a more advanced level of game customization by directly modifying the implementation code.

Specifically, we'll change the condition that triggers the game over from two cycles of the mathematical functions to three.

Changing the Game Over Condition

The game currently ends after the list of prepared functions is displayed twice. To change this to three times, you need to modify the part of the code that checks for this condition.

Locate the Procedure:

The relevant code is in the Timer1Timer procedure. This is where the game's main loop is located, and it includes the logic for updating the game state.

Find the Specific Code:

Inside the Timer1Timer procedure, look for the section that checks how many times the functions have been repeated. It will be a conditional statement (an if statement) that involves the FunctionRepeatCount variable.

Make the Change:

In this conditional statement, you will find a line similar to if FunctionRepeatCount >= 2 then. Change the 2 to 3. This alteration means that the game will now check if the functions have been repeated three times instead of two before triggering the game over condition.

Example Code Modification

```
procedure TForm1.Timer1Timer(Sender: TObject);
begin
  // ... [other code] ...

  // Check if the functions have been repeated three times
  if FunctionRepeatCount >= 3 then
  begin
    GameOver := True;
    // ... [rest of the game over logic] ...
  end;

  // ... [rest of the Timer1Timer code] ...
```

Important Notes

After making this change, it's crucial to compile the program to check for any syntactical errors. Even a small typo can cause errors.

Use the "Compile" or "Run" option in Lazarus to build the project and check for errors.

If the compilation is successful and there are no errors, run the program to see the changes in effect.

By increasing the number of function cycles before the game ends, you can make the game last longer and provide a slightly more extended experience for the player.

This kind of adjustment is a great way to understand the impact of game logic on the overall gameplay.

Advanced Level Game Adjustment:

Adding Three Graphs

In this section, we will walk through the process of adding three specific mathematical graphs to the game. This involves modifying the Const section to include new array elements and texts, updating the CalculateY function with new logic, and then compiling and visually checking the program.

Below Three functions are going to be added:

Cosine function

Y = 200 * Cos(0.02 * X)

Sine curve on Y = a*X   //a : const

Y = 0.3 * X + 100 * Sin(0.03 * X)

Sine curve on Y = a / X   // a : const

Y = 7000 / X + 20 * Sin(0.03 * X)

Step 1: Modifying the Const Section

First, we need to extend the GraphFunctions and FunctionTexts arrays in the Const section to include the new functions.

Below Bold characters were added or changed to the code

```
// Array of mathematical functions represented in the game.
GraphFunctions: array[0..7] of Integer = (0, 1, 2, 3, 4, 5, 6, 7 );
FunctionTexts: array[0..7] of string = (
  'Y = 0.0077 * X^2 - 150', // Quadratic function.
  'Y = |0.5 * X + 100|', // Absolute value function.
  'Y = 150 * Sin(0.03 * X)', // Sine function.
  'Y = 9000 / X (X ≠ 0)', // Inverse function.
  'Y = 10 * tan(0.0099 * X) (cos(0.0099X) ≠ 0)' , //
Tangent function.
  'Y = 200 * Cos(0.02 * X)', // Cosine function.
  'Y = 0.3 * X + 100 * Sin( 0.03 * X )', // 100Sin(0.03X)
on Y=0.3X
  'Y = 7000 / X + 20 * Sin( 0.03 * X )' // 10Sin(0.03X)
on 7000/X
  );
```

Step 2: Updating the CalculateY Function

Next, we add the logic for the new functions in the CalculateY function.

Below Bold characters were added to the code

```
// Calculates the Y-coordinate for the current function based on
the given X-coordinate.

function TForm1.CalculateY(X: Integer): Integer;
```

```
// The function is determined by the current function index.

case GraphFunctions[CurrentFunctionIndex] of

    0: Result := Round(0.0077 * Power(X, 2)-150);
    1: Result := Round(Abs(0.5 * X +100 ));
    2: Result := Round(150 * Sin(0.03 * X));
    3: if X <> 0 then
           //Result := Round(7000 / X)
           Result := Round(9000 / X)
       else
           Result := 0;
    4: if Cos(0.0099 * X) <> 0 then
           Result := Round(10*Sin(0.0099 * X) / Cos(0.0099
* X))
       else
           Result := 0;

    5: Result := Round(200 * cos(0.02 * X));
    6: Result := Round(0.3*X+100*sin(0.03 * X)) ;
    7: Result := Round(7000/X + 20 *sin(0.03 * X)) ;

    else
      Result := 0;
    end;

    Result := - Result; // From1's Y direction is downward

end;
```

When dealing with trigonometric functions like Y = Sin(X) in my game, it's important to consider both amplitude and period.

While the amplitude is straightforward and follows the axis markings, the period requires careful attention.

Firstly, in the game's XY coordinate plane, an increase of 1 in either X or Y corresponds to an increase of 1 pixel on the screen.

Additionally, when plotting Y = Sin(X), the X value is in radians, as per the radian measure used in trigonometry.

This means the period is 2π (two times Pi), which equals approximately 6.28. This value is quite small relative to the screen dimensions.

Therefore, to adjust the period, we need to modify the function accordingly. For instance, if we want an amplitude of 250 and a period of 1/100th of the normal period, we would write the function as

Y = 250 * Sin(0.01 * X)

This setting results in a period of

100 * 2π = 100 * 2 * 3.14 = 628

spanning 628 pixels on the screen for one complete cycle of the sine wave.

If we wish to double this period, the function would be adjusted to

Y = 250 * Sin(2 * 0.01 * X)

In this case, the period becomes 314, meaning one complete cycle of the sine wave would span 314 pixels on the screen.

These adjustments allow for the proper scaling and visualization of trigonometric functions within the game's graphical interface, ensuring that the functions are both visually appealing and mathematically accurate.

Appendix Introduction:

Your Comprehensive Lazarus and Pascal Guide

Welcome to the appendix of this book – a comprehensive repository and reference guide that transforms from a beginner's handbook to a mid-level programmer's companion in your journey with Lazarus and Pascal programming.

Purpose of the Appendix

This appendix is not just an add-on; it's a crucial part of your learning toolkit. As you progress through the main content of the book, you'll find that programming, much like any other language, has its intricacies and nuances. The appendix is designed to serve as your go-to resource, akin to a detailed dictionary or encyclopedia, for all things related to Lazarus and Pascal.

From Basics to Beyond

Whether you are a student tackling a programming assignment, a teacher looking for reference material, or a self-learner exploring new areas, this appendix aims to be your faithful companion. Starting from the very basics of Pascal grammar, it gradually delves into more complex topics. You'll find explanations on syntax, detailed descriptions of data types, variables, control structures, standard functions, and procedures – all tailored to enhance your understanding of Lazarus and Pascal.

How to Use This Appendix

As a Reference Guide:

Treat this appendix as a quick-reference guide. Stuck on a particular function or syntax? Jump into the relevant section here for clarification.

For In-Depth Understanding:

Each entry is designed to not just define a term but to also give you context – how it's used, why it's important, and where you might encounter it while programming.

For Teachers and Students:

This appendix can be a valuable educational resource. Teachers can use it to supplement teaching materials, and students can refer to it for a deeper understanding of concepts covered in class or in the main text of this book.

Continuous Learning:

As you grow in your programming skills, the appendix remains relevant. It's structured to provide more advanced information as your knowledge expands, making it suitable for users who progress to intermediate levels.

A Living Document

Lastly, it's important to note that this appendix is a 'living document'. As the world of programming evolves, so will the contents of this guide. It's tailored to grow with you, adapting to changes and incorporating new advancements in Lazarus and Pascal.

In conclusion, whether you're deciphering a complex piece of code, looking for best practices, or seeking deeper insights into Lazarus and Pascal, this appendix is your reliable resource. It's here to support your journey through the fascinating world of programming, ensuring that learning is not just effective, but also enjoyable.

Pascal and Lazarus: An Overview

Lazarus is an open-source development environment that extends the functionality of Pascal, a programming language known for its clear syntax and structured approach. While Pascal, developed by Niklaus Wirth in the 1970s, emphasizes readability and ease of understanding, Lazarus builds on these principles to provide a modern graphical interface for application development.

Pascal Grammar Basics

At the core of Pascal's language structure is its grammar, which dictates how commands, functions, and procedures are formulated. The grammar is distinguished by its use of syntax, variables, data types, control structures, and subprograms.

Syntax:

The syntax in Pascal is a set of predefined rules that determine the arrangement of symbols and text for the program to be correctly compiled and executed. It includes the way commands are structured, how variables are declared, and the format of control structures.

216

Variables:

Variables in Pascal are symbolic names representing memory locations. Each variable is associated with a data type, and its value can be changed throughout the program. For example, declaring personAge: Integer; creates an integer variable named personAge.

Data Types:

Pascal supports various data types, including integers, real (floating-point numbers), characters, and more complex types like arrays and records. For instance, person[1].age := 18; sets the age field of the first element in a person array record to 18.

Common Controls:

Control structures like if, while, for, and with are used for decision-making and controlling the flow of the program. For example, if (personAge > 18) then writeln('Adult'); checks if personAge is greater than 18 and outputs "Adult" if true.

Procedures and Functions:

These are subprograms in Pascal. A procedure performs a task but does not return a value, whereas a function performs a task and returns a value. They help in breaking down complex problems into simpler, reusable blocks.

Lazarus: Enhancing Pascal

Lazarus leverages these aspects of Pascal to provide a more accessible and powerful environment for software development. It includes an Integrated Development Environment (IDE) that simplifies coding, debugging, and designing graphical user interfaces. With Lazarus, developers can create applications that run on various platforms, enhancing the versatility of Pascal in modern programming contexts.

Arithmetic Operators

Arithmetic operators are used to perform basic mathematical operations.

Addition (+): Adds two values.

Example: X + Y adds X and Y.
If X = 5 and Y = 3, then X + Y equals 8.

Subtraction (-): Subtracts one value from another.

Example: X - Y subtracts Y from X.
If X = 5 and Y = 3, then X - Y equals 2.

Multiplication (*): Multiplies two values.

Example: X * Y multiplies X and Y.
If X = 5 and Y = 3, then X * Y equals 15.

Division (/): Divides one value by another.

Example: X / Y divides X by Y.
If X = 15 and Y = 3, then X / Y equals 5.

Modulus (mod): Finds the remainder of the division of one number by another.

Example: X mod Y gives the remainder when X is divided by Y. If X = 17 and Y = 5, then X mod Y equals 2 (since 17 divided by 5 is 3 remainder 2).

Comparison Operators

Comparison operators are used to compare two values.

Equal to (=): Checks if two values are equal.

Example: X = Y checks if X and Y are equal. If X = 5 and Y = 5, then X = Y is True.

Not equal to (<>): Checks if two values are not equal.

Example: X <> Y checks if X and Y are not equal. If X = 5 and Y = 3, then X <> Y is True.

Greater than (>): Checks if one value is greater than another.

Example: X > Y checks if X is greater than Y. If X = 6 and Y = 3, then X > Y is True.

Less than (<): Checks if one value is less than another.

Example: X < Y checks if X is less than Y. If X = 2 and Y = 5, then X < Y is True.

Greater than or equal to (>=): Checks if one value is greater than or equal to another.

Example: X >= Y checks if X is greater than or equal to Y.
If X = 5 and Y = 5, then X >= Y is True.

Less than or equal to (<=): Checks if one value is less than or equal to another.

Example: X <= Y checks if X is less than or equal to Y.
If X = 3 and Y = 5, then X <= Y is True.

Logical Operators

Logical operators are used to combine conditional statements.

AND (and): True if both statements are true.

Example: X > 5 and Y < 10 is True if X is greater than 5 and Y is less than 10.

OR (or): True if at least one of the statements is true.

Example: X < 5 or Y > 10 is True if X is less than 5 or Y is greater than 10.

NOT (not): True if the statement is false.

Example: not(X > 5) is True if X is not greater than 5.
Using Operators in Expressions

Operators can be combined to form expressions. Expressions are used to compute values, make decisions, and control the flow of a program.

Example of a complex expression: (X + Y) * Z > 10 and W = 5. This checks if the result of multiplying the sum of X and Y with Z is greater than 10 and if W equals 5.

Comments

Single-Line Comment (//):

Purpose:

Used to add explanatory notes or to temporarily disable code.

Syntax:

// Your comment here

Example:
// This is a single-line comment
X := 5; // This sets X to 5

Multi-Line Comment ({ and }):

Purpose:

Used for longer comments that span multiple lines or to comment out blocks of code.

Syntax:

{ Your comment here } or (* Your comment here *)

Example:

```
{
  This is a multi-line comment.
  It can span several lines.
}
```

(* This is also a multi-line comment. *)
End of Statement

Semicolon (;):

Purpose: Used to mark the end of a statement or command.

Syntax: statement;

Example:

```
X := 10;
Y := X + 5;
```

Note: In Pascal, the semicolon is a statement separator rather than a terminator, which means the last statement before an end or a block does not strictly require a semicolon. However, it's good practice to use it consistently for clarity.

Other Important Syntax Elements

Colon (:):

Used in variable declarations to separate the variable name from its type.

Example:
```
var
  X: Integer;
```

Assignment Operator (=):

Used to assign a value to a variable.

Example:

X := 5;   // Assigns the value 5 to X

Dot (.) :

Used to access fields of a record or properties/methods of an object. And it is used at the end of the program.

Example:

MyRecord.Field := 10;
MyObject.Method();

Comma (,):

Used to separate items in a list, such as parameters in a method call or elements in an array.

Example:

procedure MyProcedure(X, Y: Integer);
Parentheses (()):

Used to group expressions or to enclose parameters in method calls.

Example:

Z := (X + Y) * 2;
MyProcedure(X, Y);

Square Brackets [ ]:

Used to specify array indices or set elements.

Example:

224

```
MyArray[3] := 10;
MySet := [1, 2, 3, 4];
```

Begin and End:

Used to start and end a block of code, especially in compound statements like if, while, or for loops.

Example:

```
if X > 5 then
begin
    Y := X + 10;
    Z := Y - 2;
end;
```

Understanding these basic elements is key to writing clear and functional Pascal code in Lazarus. They form the foundation of the language's syntax and are used in almost every Pascal program.

Integer Types:

Integer: General-purpose integer.

LongInt: Larger integer.

ShortInt: Smaller range integer.

Byte: Unsigned integer (0-255).

Floating-Point Types:

Real: General floating-point number.

Double: Double-precision floating-point.

Single: Single-precision floating-point.

Real:

This is a general floating-point type. Its precision and range can vary depending on the compiler and platform but is usually less precise than Double.

Double:

This type represents a double-precision floating-point number. It offers a larger range and more precision than Real. It's commonly used when high numerical precision is needed.

Single:

This type stands for single-precision floating-point numbers. It has less precision than Double and is used when you need more precision than Real but want to save memory compared to Double.

String and Character Types:

String: A string of characters.

Char: A single character.

Boolean Type:

Boolean: Logical type (True/False).

Composite Types:

Array: Ordered collection of elements.

Record: Collection of mixed data types.

Pointer Types:

Pointer: Generic pointer type.

Dynamic Array:

Dynamic array: Array whose size can change at runtime.

Sample Code:

Integer Types:

Integer:

```
var
  MyInt: Integer; MyInt := 10;
```

LongInt:

```
var
  MyLongInt: LongInt; MyLongInt := 100000;
```

ShortInt:

```
var
  MyShortInt: ShortInt; MyShortInt := 127;
```

Byte:

```
var
  MyByte: Byte; MyByte := 255;
```

Floating-Point Types:

Real:

```
var
  MyReal: Real;
  MyReal := 3.14;
```

Double:

```
var
  MyDouble: Double;
```

```
    MyDouble := 123.456;
```

Single:

```
var
   MySingle: Single;
   MySingle := 1.23;
```

String and Character Types:

String:

```
var
   MyString: String;
   MyString := 'Hello';
```

Char:

```
var
   MyChar: Char;
   MyChar := 'A';
```

Boolean Type:

Boolean:

```
var
   MyBool: Boolean;
   MyBool := True;
```

Composite Types:

Array:

```
var
   MyArray: array[1..5] of Integer;
   MyArray[1] := 10;
```

229

Record:

```
type
  MyRecord = record
      Age: Integer;
      Name: String;
  end;

var
  Person: MyRecord;
```

**This is another sample: Types + Array

```
type
  PersonRecord = record
    Age: Integer;
    Name, City, FavoriteFood: String;
  end;

var
  People: array[1..3] of PersonRecord;
  i: Integer;

begin
  // Assigning values to each person in the array
  People[1].Age := 30;
  People[1].Name := 'Alice';
  People[1].City := 'New York';
  People[1].FavoriteFood := 'Pizza';

  People[2].Age := 25;
  People[2].Name := 'Bob';
  People[2].City := 'London';
  People[2].FavoriteFood := 'Pasta';

  People[3].Age := 35;
  People[3].Name := 'Charlie';
  People[3].City := 'Paris';
  People[3].FavoriteFood := 'Sushi';

  // Displaying the information for each person
  for i := 1 to 3 do
  begin
```

```
      writeln('Person ', i, ':');
      writeln('   Name          : ', People[i].Name);
      writeln('   Age           : ', People[i].Age);
      writeln('   City          : ', People[i].City);
      writeln('   Favorite Food : ', People[i].FavoriteFood);
      writeln;
  end;
end;
```

Pointer Types:

Pointer: *****caution for using pointer

```
var
   MyPointer: Pointer;
   New(MyPointer);
```

Dynamic Array:

```
var
   MyDynamicArray: array of Integer;
   SetLength(MyDynamicArray, 5);
   MyDynamicArray[0] := 1;
```

*****caution for using pointer functionality

For beginners and intermediate Lazarus programmers, explicit control over pointers is typically not required.

This is more in the domain of advanced programming. A key advantage of Lazarus (Pascal) is that it abstracts many of the complexities associated with direct memory management.

In the background, Lazarus and the operating system handle memory allocation and pointer management, reducing the burden on the programmer.

However, Lazarus (Pascal) does offer the capability to control pointers for those who reach an advanced level of programming.

Properly handling, controlling, and debugging pointers requires a comprehensive understanding of what pointers are and how they are used.

I recommend that beginners and intermediate users focus on the rich features and high-level programming capabilities of Lazarus before delving into pointer control.

This approach aligns well with the educational and user-friendly nature of Lazarus. My 2D game programming, for instance, is designed without explicit use of pointers, demonstrating the effectiveness of this methodology.

Advanced users can explore pointer functionality as they become more comfortable with the core aspects of the language and IDE.

In Lazarus and Pascal, there are specific rules and conventions for naming variables that beginners should be aware of.

Understanding these rules is crucial to avoid syntax errors and to write clear, maintainable code.

Here's a summary of the key rules and some additional points of consideration:

Start with a Letter:

Variable names must begin with a letter (either uppercase A-Z or lowercase a-z). They cannot start with a digit or any special character.

✅ Correct: X12, x2024
✖ Incorrect: 12X, 2024X

Alphanumeric and Underscores:

After the initial letter, variable names can include letters, digits (0-9), and underscores (_). No other special characters or spaces are allowed.

✅ Examples: my_var, counter1, data_2023

Case Sensitivity:

Unlike C or C++, Pascal is not case-sensitive. This means that XYZ12, xYZ12, and xyz12 are all considered the same variable name. In languages like C, these would be distinct variables.

Avoid Reserved Words:

Do not use reserved words (like begin, end, var, etc.) as variable names.

✖ Incorrect: var := 5;, begin := 10;

233

Additional Considerations

Length:

Pascal variable names can be quite lengthy, but it's good practice to choose concise yet descriptive names.

Readability:

Use names that clearly describe the purpose of the variable. For example, userAge is more descriptive than just a.

Conventions:

Although Pascal is not case-sensitive, many developers use specific conventions like CamelCase or snake_case for readability and consistency.

In Lazarus and Pascal, there are certain reserved words that have a predefined meaning in the language and thus cannot be used as names for variables, constants, types, or other identifiers.

These words are integral to the syntax and structure of the language. Here's a list of some of the most common reserved words in Pascal, which are also relevant in the Lazarus environment:

and
array
begin
case
const
div
do
downto
else
end
file
for
function
goto
if
implementation
in
inline
interface
label
mod
nil
not
object
of
on
operator
or
packed

procedure
program
record
reintroduce
repeat
set
shl
shr
string
then
to
type
unit
until
uses
var
while
with
xor

It's important for beginners to understand that these words have special meanings and uses in Pascal, and should not be used for naming their own variables or identifiers.

This is a standard practice in many programming languages, where certain words are reserved for language operations and constructs.

If Statement:

Used for conditional execution of code.

Syntax:
  if condition then statement;

Can be extended with else for alternative actions.

Case Statement:

Selects one of many code blocks to execute.

Syntax:
  case variable of
    value1: statement1;
    value2: statement2; ...
  end;

For Loop:

Repeats a block of code a specified number of times.

Syntax:
  for variable := start to end do statement;
to can be replaced with down to for decreasing sequences.

While Loop:

Continues executing as long as a condition is true.

Syntax:
  while condition do
    statement;

Repeat-Until Loop:

Similar to while, but checks the condition at the end of the loop.

Syntax:
  repeat statement; until condition;

With Statement:

Simplifies code when accessing the properties of an object.

Syntax:
  with object do statement;

Sample code:

If-Else Statement

```
var
  age: Integer;
begin
  age := 15;
  if age >= 13 then
  begin
    writeln('You are a teenager.');
  end
  else
  begin
    writeln('You are not a teenager.');
  end;
end;
```

Case Statement:

```
var
  grade: Char;
begin
  grade := 'A';
  case grade of
    'A': writeln('Excellent!');
    'B': writeln('Very Good');
    // ... other cases ...
  end;
end;
```

For Loop:

```
var
  i: Integer;
begin
  for i := 1 to 5 do
  begin
```

```pascal
      writeln('Number: ', i);
   end;
end;


** this code is also correct
**IntToStr() changes the data Integer To String

var
   i: Integer;
begin
   for i := 1 to 5 do
   begin
     writeln('Number: ' + IntToStr(i));
   end;
end;
```

While Loop:

```pascal
var
   count: Integer;
begin
   count := 1;
   while count <= 5 do
   begin
     writeln('Count: ', count);
     count := count + 1;
   end;
end;
```

Repeat-Until Loop:

```pascal
var
   count: Integer;
begin
   count := 1;
   repeat
     writeln('Count: ', count);
     count := count + 1;
   until count > 5;
end;
```

With Statement:

```
type
  TCar = record
    make: String;
    year: Integer;
  end;
var
  myCar: TCar;
begin
  myCar.make := 'Toyota';
  myCar.year := 2020;
  with myCar do
  begin
    writeln('Car: ', make, ', Year: ', year);
  end;
end;
```

File Menu

New:

Allows you to create a new project, unit, form, or other file types.

Open:

Opens an existing file or project.

Save:

Saves the current file.

Save As:

Saves the current file with a new name.

Save All:

Saves all open files in the current project.

Close:

Closes the current file.

Close All:

Closes all open files.

242

Quit:

Exits the Lazarus IDE.

Edit Menu

Undo:

Reverts the last action.

Redo:

Reapplies an action that was undone.

Cut:

Removes the selected text and places it on the clipboard.

Copy:

Copies the selected text to the clipboard.

Paste:

Inserts text from the clipboard at the cursor position.

View Menu

Toggle Form/Unit View:

This feature is extremely useful, especially for beginners who are working with forms (Graphical User Interface).

In Lazarus, each form has an associated unit (code file) where the logic is written. The "Toggle Form/Unit View" option allows you to switch between the visual design of the form and its underlying Pascal code.

Project Menu

New Project:

Starts a new project, offering a variety of project types to choose from.

Open Project:

Opens an existing Lazarus project file (.lpi).

Save Project:

Saves the current project.

Save Project As:

Saves the current project with a new name.

Project Options:

Provides options to configure your project, such as compiler settings, paths, and application information.

Run Menu

Compile:

Compiling is the process of converting the Pascal source code into an executable program. When you select "Compile", Lazarus checks your code for syntax errors and logical issues. If there are any errors, they are displayed in the messages window, allowing you to identify and fix them before running the program.

Run:

When you choose "Run > Run" in Lazarus, it launches your application within the Lazarus integrated debugger. This allows the IDE to monitor the execution of your program and interact with it in real-time.

Pause:

Pauses the execution of your program during debugging.

Stop:

Stops the running or debugging of your application.

Step Over:

Executes the current line of code and moves to the next one during debugging.

Tools Menu

Options:

General IDE options and settings, such as editor preferences, environment options, etc.

Build Lazarus with Profile:

Compiles the Lazarus IDE itself with specific build profiles.

Window Menu

Cascade:

Arranges all open editor and form windows in a cascading manner.

Tile:

Tiles all open windows within the IDE.

Close All Editor Windows:

Closes all open editor windows.

Help Menu

Online Help:

Opens the online help documentation for Lazarus.

About Lazarus:

Displays information about your Lazarus IDE version and other relevant details.

Compile by Lazarus

The "Compile" option under the Run menu is an essential part of the development process in Lazarus.

It allows you to compile your code without running the application. Compiling is the process of converting the Pascal source code into an executable program.

When you select "Compile", Lazarus checks your code for syntax errors and logical issues. If there are any errors, they are displayed in the messages window, allowing you to identify and fix them before running the program.

This step is crucial because it ensures that your code is free of errors that would prevent it from running correctly. It's a best practice to compile your code frequently as you write it to catch errors early in the development process.

For beginners, regularly compiling code is a good habit to develop. It helps you understand the importance of writing error-free code and familiarizes you with common mistakes and how to resolve them.

Run by Lazarus

The "Run > Run" command in Lazarus is a crucial part of the development process, particularly when testing and debugging your application. Here's an explanation of what it does and how it differs from simply clicking the executable file.

What "Run > Run" Does:

Starts the Application Within the Debugger:

When you choose "Run > Run" in Lazarus, it launches your application within the Lazarus integrated debugger. This allows the IDE to monitor the execution of your program and interact with it in real-time.

Debugging Capabilities:

Running your application in this mode enables various debugging capabilities. You can set breakpoints, step through your code line by line, inspect variables, and watch expressions. This helps in identifying and fixing logical errors and bugs that are not apparent just by looking at the code.

Error and Exception Handling:

If your program encounters any runtime errors or exceptions, the debugger will pause execution and highlight the problematic line of code. This immediate feedback is invaluable for understanding and resolving issues that may not be evident through compilation alone.

Difference from Clicking the Executable:

Running Outside the Debugger(only click the exe file) :

When you directly click the executable file generated by Lazarus, the program runs outside the Lazarus environment. This means you don't have access to the debugging tools provided by the IDE, such as breakpoints and variable inspection.

Real-world Environment Testing:

Executing the standalone file is similar to how the end-user will run your application. It's a good practice to test your program in this manner to ensure it behaves as expected in a real-world scenario, outside the development environment.

Limited Error Handling:

Without the debugger, if your application encounters an error, it may crash or behave unexpectedly without providing detailed information about the cause. This makes troubleshooting more challenging.

STANDARD TAB COMPONENTS

TMainMenu

Description:

A menu component that creates a traditional menu bar at the top of an application window. It's used for organizing and grouping commands and features like 'File', 'Edit', 'View', etc.

Usage:

Essential for applications requiring a structured menu system, providing users with a familiar and intuitive way to navigate and access various functionalities.

TPopupMenu

Description:

A context menu that appears upon user interaction, typically a right-click. It offers a list of options and actions relevant to the current context or element.

Usage:

Useful for providing additional options, shortcuts, or functionalities that are relevant to specific components or areas within your application.

TButton

Description:

A clickable button used to initiate an action or command. It's a fundamental component in GUI applications for user interaction.

Usage:

Ideal for triggering events like form submission, opening a dialog box, starting a process, or any interactive function.

TLabel

Description: A non-editable text element used for displaying labels, instructions, or information next to other components like input fields.

Usage:

Commonly paired with input controls to provide descriptions or guidance, enhancing the clarity and user-friendliness of your application's interface.

TEdit

Description: A single-line text input field allowing users to enter and edit text. It's one of the basic elements for user input in forms.

Usage: Used for gathering simple input like names, email addresses, search queries, etc., where a single line of text is sufficient.

TMemo

Description:

A multiline text editor that allows users to enter, display, and edit longer texts. It expands the capabilities of TEdit for handling more text.

Usage:

Ideal for cases where you need to handle paragraphs of text, such as a comments section, text editor, or any application requiring extensive text input.

TToggleBox

Description:

A checkable button that represents an on/off state. It's similar to TCheckBox but styled like a button.

Usage:

Great for options or settings that can be toggled, such as enabling/disabling features in your application.

TCheckBox

Description:

A small box that can be checked or unchecked, representing a binary choice.

Usage:

Commonly used in forms and settings for enabling or disabling options, or for making multiple selections from a set of choices.

TRadioButton

Description:

Allows users to select a single option from a group of choices, ensuring that only one option can be selected at a time.

Usage:

Best suited for presenting a set of mutually exclusive choices, like selecting a gender, a payment method, or any scenario where only one choice is valid.

TListBox

Description:

Displays a list of items, allowing users to select one or more items from the list. It's a basic element for presenting lists of data.

Usage:

Useful for scenarios where you need to present a list of items for selection, like a list of files, settings, or any list-based interaction.

TComboBox

Description:

Combines the functionality of an editable text field and a drop-down list, allowing users to either select an item from a predefined list or enter a new value.

Usage:

Ideal for inputs where the user can either choose from a set of standard options or input a custom value, like selecting a country or typing a new one.

TScrollBar

Description:

A control for scrolling through content that is too long or wide to fit within its visible area, like text or images.

Usage:

Essential for adding scrolling capability to forms or components containing content that exceeds the display area.

TGroupBox

Description:

A container with an optional caption for grouping related controls, enhancing the organizational structure of forms.

Usage:

Used for visually grouping and segregating related UI elements, such as radio buttons or checkboxes that fall under a common category.

TRadioGroup

Description:

A group of radio buttons that behave as a single unit, ensuring only one selection within the group.

Usage:

Convenient for scenarios where multiple radio buttons are required, simplifying the process of creating and managing them.

TCheckGroup

Description:

Similar to TRadioGroup but for checkboxes, allowing multiple selections within the group.

Usage:

Perfect for situations where you need a group of checkboxes that are related, like selecting multiple options from a set.

TPanel

Description:

A versatile container control used to group other controls or organize sections of a form.

Usage:

Useful for dividing forms into logical sections or for custom layout designs, adding structure to your application's interface.

TActionList

Description:

Manages a collection of actions that can be linked to various UI elements like menus and toolbars.

Usage:

Useful for centralizing the event handling logic, especially in applications with complex interfaces.

TBitBtn

Description:

A button that can display both text and images. It's an enhancement over the standard TButton, providing more visual flexibility.

Usage:

Ideal for toolbar buttons or any control where you want to combine text with icons for a more intuitive and visually appealing interface.

TSpeedButton

Description:

A button designed for use on toolbars, offering fast access to certain functions. Unlike TButton, it does not take focus when clicked, making it better suited for toolbars.

Usage:

Perfect for creating a set of quick-action buttons in your application, such as play, pause, stop buttons in a media player.

TStaticText

Description:

Similar to TLabel, but offers additional features like 3D effects and the ability to align text.

257

Usage:

Useful when you want a label with more stylistic options or when you need to display text in a non-standard alignment.

TImage

Description:

A component for displaying images in various formats. You can load images at design time or runtime.

Usage:

Essential for showing graphics, photos, icons, or any visual content in your application. Can be used for backgrounds, icons, or as part of the UI.

TShape

Description:

Draws simple geometric shapes (like rectangles, circles, and lines) on a form. It's useful for decorative and organizational purposes in the UI.

Usage:

Can be used to create visual separators, backgrounds, or just to add visual appeal to the user interface.

TBevel

Description:

A component that draws a single line or a raised or sunken rectangular frame on a form, often used for visual grouping or as a separator.

Usage:

Ideal for creating visual distinctions between different sections of a user interface without the need for full panels or group boxes.

TPaintBox

Description:

A blank control used for custom drawing. You can use it to draw graphics programmatically.

Usage:

Perfect for custom graphics, animations, or when you need to draw shapes, text, or images in a more controlled way than standard components allow.

TNotebook

Description:

A component that contains multiple pages, similar to a physical notebook. Each page can contain other controls.

Usage:

Useful for organizing content that needs to be grouped but not necessarily visible all at once, like a multi-step form.

TLabeledEdit

Description:

Combines an edit box with a permanently associated label in one control, simplifying the layout process.

Usage:

Ideal for forms where each text input needs a corresponding label, making your forms cleaner and reducing the need for separate TLabel controls.

TSplitter

Description:

A control that allows the user to dynamically resize adjacent controls at runtime, like panels or windows.

Usage:

Great for creating adjustable user interfaces where the user can decide how much space each part of the interface should occupy.

TTrayIcon

Description:

Allows your application to place an icon in the system tray. It can be used to show notifications or provide quick access to common functions.

Usage:

Useful for applications that need to run in the background or provide notifications, like a mail client or a system monitor tool.

TMaskEdit

Description:

An edit control that restricts input to a specific format or pattern, like a phone number or date.

Usage:

Essential for forms requiring structured input where the data must follow a particular format, ensuring data consistency and reducing input errors.

TCheckListBox

Description:

A combination of a list box and checkboxes, allowing for multiple items in the list to be selected via checkboxes.

Usage:

Ideal for settings, options, or any situation where you need to present a list of items with selectable options.

TScrollBox

Description:

A container control with its own scrollbars, useful for holding other controls that might exceed the available viewing area.

Usage:

Perfect for creating scrollable areas in your application, especially when you have more content or controls than can fit on the screen.

TApplicationProperties

Description:

Provides a centralized way to handle various application-wide properties and events, like user actions or system messages.

Usage:

Useful for managing global settings and behaviors in your application, such as how it responds to certain system events.

TStringGrid

Description:

A grid control that displays items in a tabular format, similar to a spreadsheet. Each cell can contain text.

Usage:

Ideal for displaying and managing tabular data, especially when you need a simple way to show and edit data in a grid format.

TDrawGrid

Description:

A customizable grid control where each cell can be individually drawn, offering more control than TStringGrid.

Usage:

Best suited for applications requiring a grid with custom drawing in cells, like a chess game or a custom data visualization tool.

TPairSplitter

Description:

A control that contains two panels separated by a splitter, allowing the user to adjust the size of the panels.

Usage:

Great for interfaces where you want to give the user control over the layout, such as adjusting the width of a sidebar relative to the main content area.

TColorBox

Description:

A drop-down list that displays a list of colors and allows the user to select a color.

Usage:

Perfect for any application where the user needs to select a color, like a drawing tool or a customization option in a settings menu.

TColorListBox

Description:

Similar to TColorBox but displayed as a list box, showing more colors at once.

Usage:

Ideal when you want to present a larger palette of colors to choose from in a single view, such as in a graphic editing application.

TTrackBar

Description:

A slider control allowing users to select a value by moving a slider along a track. It's used for inputting numerical values within a specified range.

Usage:

Ideal for settings that require a range of values, like adjusting volume or brightness. It offers a more interactive and intuitive way for users to input values compared to entering them manually.

TProgressBar

Description:

Displays the progress of an operation as a bar filling up over time. It's useful for giving visual feedback during lengthy processes.

Usage:

Commonly used in scenarios where the user needs to be informed about the progress of a task, such as file uploads, downloads, or installation processes.

TTreeView

Description:

Presents items in a hierarchical tree structure, allowing for expandable and collapsible nodes.

Usage:

Essential for applications that need to display data in a hierarchical manner, such as file explorers, organizational charts, or settings with nested categories.

TListView

Description:

A versatile control that displays a list of items in various formats like report, list, and icon views.

Usage:

Perfect for applications that need to display lists of items with additional details, such as file lists, email inboxes, or product catalogs.

TStatusBar

Description:

A horizontal bar typically displayed at the bottom of a window, used to display various kinds of status information.

Usage:

Ideal for showing brief messages, hints, or status information like connection status, progress updates, or contextual tips.

TToolBar

Description:

Provides a row of clickable buttons or icons, usually located at the top of an application window, for quick access to common functions.

Usage:

Great for applications that require a set of frequently used actions to be readily accessible, such as text editors, browsers, or graphic design tools.

TUpDown

Description:

A pair of vertical or horizontal arrows used for incrementing or decrementing a value, commonly associated with an edit box.

Usage:

Useful in scenarios where the user needs to adjust a numerical value in small increments, like setting a quantity or adjusting a measurement.

TPageControl

Description:

A component that contains multiple tabbed pages, allowing the user to switch between different views or settings within the same window.

Usage:

Perfect for organizing content into separate, easily navigable sections, such as in configuration dialogs or multi-section forms.

TTabControl

Description:

Similar to TPageControl, but only the tabs are displayed. The content for each tab needs to be managed separately.

Usage:

Ideal for scenarios where you want greater control over the content displayed with each tab, or when integrating with other custom controls.

THeaderControl

Description:

Displays a header with resizable and clickable sections, often used in conjunction with list views or custom layouts.

Usage:

Useful for creating interactive headers in data display controls, allowing users to resize or reorder columns, such as in a file manager or data grid.

TImageList

Description:

Manages a collection of images for use in other components, ensuring consistent and optimized image handling.

Usage:

Essential for applications that use multiple images across different controls, such as toolbars and menus, providing efficient and organized image management.

TPopupNotifier

Description:

Displays a small pop-up window to notify users, similar to a toast notification.

Essential for forms requiring structured input where the data must follow a particular format, ensuring data consistency and reducing input errors.

TCheckListBox

Description:

A combination of a list box and checkboxes, allowing for multiple items in the list to be selected via checkboxes.

Usage:

Ideal for settings, options, or any situation where you need to present a list of items with selectable options.

TScrollBox

Description:
A container control with its own scrollbars, useful for holding other controls that might exceed the available viewing area.

Usage:

Perfect for creating scrollable areas in your application, especially when you have more content or controls than can fit on the screen.

TApplicationProperties

Description:

Provides a centralized way to handle various application-wide properties and events, like user actions or system messages.

Usage:

Useful for managing global settings and behaviors in your application, such as how it responds to certain system events.

TStringGrid

Description:

A grid control that displays items in a tabular format, similar to a spreadsheet. Each cell can contain text.

Usage:

Ideal for displaying and managing tabular data, especially when you need a simple way to show and edit data in a grid format.

TDrawGrid

Description:

A customizable grid control where each cell can be individually drawn, offering more control than TStringGrid.

Usage:

Best suited for applications requiring a grid with custom drawing in cells, like a chess game or a custom data visualization tool.

TPairSplitter

Description:

A control that contains two panels separated by a splitter, allowing the user to adjust the size of the panels.

Usage:

Great for interfaces where you want to give the user control over the layout, such as adjusting the width of a sidebar relative to the main content area.

TColorBox

Description:

A drop-down list that displays a list of colors and allows the user to select a color.

Usage:

Perfect for any application where the user needs to select a color, like a drawing tool or a customization option in a settings menu.

TColorListBox

Description:

Similar to TColorBox but displayed as a list box, showing more colors at once.

Usage:

Ideal when you want to present a larger palette of colors to choose from in a single view, such as in a graphic editing application.

TOpenDialog

Description:

A standard dialog that allows users to select and open files. It provides a familiar interface for navigating the file system.

Usage:

Useful for any application that needs to allow users to open files, such as text editors, media players, or image viewers.

TSaveDialog

Description:

Similar to TOpenDialog, but used for saving files. It lets users choose a location and enter a filename for saving data.

Usage:

Essential for applications where users create or edit content that they might want to save, like documents, projects, or customized settings.

TSelectDirectoryDialog

Description:

A dialog box for selecting a directory (folder) instead of a file, allowing users to browse and select a directory path.

Usage:

Ideal for applications that require users to specify a folder for operations like saving multiple files, backups, or batch processing.

TColorDialog

Description:

Presents a color picker to the user, offering various ways to choose and customize colors.

Usage:

Great for applications that involve color selection, such as graphic design tools, drawing applications, or customization features.

TFontDialog

Description:

Allows users to select a font from the system's available fonts, along with its style and size.

Usage:

Useful in text editors, word processors, or any application where text customization is a feature.

TFindDialog / TReplaceDialog

Description:

Provides standard 'Find' and 'Replace' dialog boxes for searching and replacing text.

Usage:

Essential for text-handling applications where users need to search for specific terms or replace text.

TOpenPictureDialog / TSavePictureDialog

Description:

Specialized versions of the open and save dialogs for dealing specifically with image files.

Usage:

Tailored for applications that handle images, making it easier for users to open and save picture files.

TCalendarDialog

Description:

A dialog for selecting dates using a visual calendar interface.

Usage:

Ideal for applications that require date input, such as event planners, scheduling tools, or booking systems.

TCalculatorDialog

Description:

Presents a calculator interface to the user, allowing for basic arithmetic operations.

Usage:

Useful in applications where users might need to do quick calculations without leaving the application.

TPrinterSetupDialog

Description:

Provides a dialog for configuring printer settings, such as selecting a printer and adjusting its properties.

Usage:

Essential for applications with printing capabilities, allowing users to configure their printouts.

TPrintDialog

Description:

A dialog for managing print jobs, with options like selecting the printer, number of copies, and page range.

Usage:

Useful in any application where printing documents, images, or reports is a feature.

TPageSetupDialog

Description:

Allows users to configure page settings, like margins, orientation, and paper size, for printing documents.

Usage:

Ideal for applications where the layout of printed pages is important, like word processors or report generators.

TDBNavigator

Description:

A component that provides a simple user interface for navigating through records in a database. It includes standard buttons like First, Next, Previous, Last, Add, Delete, and others.

Usage:

Ideal for database applications where users need to browse, edit, or manage records in a dataset.

TDBText

Description:

A label-like component for displaying data fields from a connected database. It updates automatically as you navigate through records.

Usage:

Useful in forms that display data from a database, particularly when you need to show read-only information from a record.

TDBEdit

Description:

An editable text field linked to a specific field in a database. Allows users to view and modify the content of the database field.

Usage:

Essential for database applications that require user input or editing of database records, like data entry forms or editing interfaces.

TDBMemo

Description:

A multi-line text editor that's connected to a database field, suitable for editing longer text data stored in the database.

Usage:

Perfect for handling large text fields in a database, such as comments, descriptions, or any extensive textual data.

TDBImage

Description:

Displays image data from a database field in a form. It supports various graphic formats stored in the database.

Usage:

Ideal for applications that need to show images stored in a database, like product catalogs, photo galleries, or user profiles.

TDBListBox

Description:

A list box component that displays a list of values from a database field. Users can select items from the list.

278

Usage:

Useful for displaying lists of database-driven options, such as categories, tags, or any selectable data from a database.

TDBComboBox

Description:

Combines a text field and a drop-down list, both linked to database fields. Allows selection from a list or entering a new value.

Usage:

Great for input forms where users can choose from a list of database-driven options or enter a new value, like selecting a product category or adding a new one.

TDBCheckBox

Description:

A checkbox linked to a Boolean field in a database, showing whether the field is true or false.

Usage:

Suitable for representing binary choices stored in a database, like active/inactive status, yes/no answers, or any true/false conditions.

TDBRadioGroup

Description:

A group of radio buttons connected to a database field, allowing selection among several options stored in the database.

Usage:

Effective for scenarios where a single choice needs to be made from database-driven options, such as selecting a payment method or status.

TDBCalendar

Description:

A calendar component for selecting dates, linked to a date field in a database. It provides a graphical interface for date selection.

Usage:

Useful for applications that require date input or selection directly from a database, like booking systems or event schedulers.

TDBGroupBox

Description:

A container component for grouping other data-aware controls, tied to fields in a database. It helps in organizing the layout of database-related controls.

Usage:

Ideal for creating structured forms with multiple data-bound controls, enhancing the clarity and organization of the user interface.

TDBGrid

Description:

Displays records from a database in a tabular grid format. It allows users to view and interact with data in a spreadsheet-like environment.

Usage:

Central to many database applications, particularly those that require viewing, sorting, or editing data in a table format, like inventory systems or customer databases.

The Data Controls tab in Lazarus is essential for developing database-driven applications.

These components make it easier to connect user interface elements directly to database fields, streamlining the process of displaying and managing data.

TDatasource

Description:

Serves as a bridge between UI components and datasets. It provides a way for data-aware components to access data from various kinds of datasets.

Usage:

Essential in any database application, as it connects the data in your application's database to the visual components on your forms.

TMemDataset

Description:

An in-memory dataset which can be used to store data temporarily during program execution. It doesn't require a database server.

Usage:

Useful for applications that need to manipulate datasets on the fly without the need for persistent storage, such as temporary data processing.

TSdfDataSet

Description:

A dataset component for working with Simple Delimited Files, like CSV. It allows reading from and writing to delimited text files. Usage:

Ideal for applications that need to interact with CSV or other delimited text files, like importing/exporting data to and from spreadsheets.

TFixedFormatDataSet

Description:

Used for datasets in a fixed format, typically text files where each field has a fixed width.

Usage:

Great for dealing with legacy data formats or interfacing with systems that output data in a fixed-width format.

TDbf

Description:

A dataset component for working with dBase files, a widely-used format for simple databases.

Usage:

Suitable for applications that need to access or manipulate data stored in dBase file format, common in older software systems.

The "Data Access" tab in Lazarus is focused on components that facilitate the access and manipulation of data in various formats.

These components are crucial for applications dealing with data storage, whether in standard databases, text files, or more specialized formats like CSV or fixed-width text files.

They provide the necessary functionality to connect, read, and write data efficiently within your Lazarus applications.

TTimer

Description:

A non-visual component that triggers an event at specified intervals. It's used to execute code repeatedly after a set amount of time.

Usage:

Ideal for periodic tasks within an application, such as updating the user interface, checking for updates, or running background processes at regular intervals.

TIdleTimer

Description:

Similar to TTimer, but triggers events when the application is idle (not processing user input or other tasks).

Usage:

Useful for tasks that should be executed during idle time, like background data processing or cleanup tasks, to avoid interfering with the user's experience.

TLazComponentQueue

Description:

A non-visual component that queues and manages the execution of methods. It helps in organizing the execution flow of your application.

Usage:

Beneficial for managing and sequencing multiple tasks or methods, especially in complex applications where task prioritization and organization are crucial.

THtmlHelpDatabase & THtmlBrowserHelpViewer

Description:

Components used for integrating HTML-based help systems into applications.

Usage:

Essential for applications that require an embedded help system or documentation, providing users with easy access to assistance and information.

TProcessUTF8 & TAsyncProcess

Description:

Components for running external processes or programs from your application. TAsyncProcess allows for non-blocking execution.

Usage:

Used when you need to run or interact with external applications or scripts from within your Lazarus application.

TProcess

Description:

A more basic variant of TProcessUTF8 for running external processes, but without UTF-8 support.

Usage:

Suitable for simpler use cases where external processes need to be executed without the need for UTF-8 encoding support.

TSimpleIPCClient & TSimpleIPCServer

Description:

Components for inter-process communication (IPC). They allow different processes to communicate with each other.

Usage:

Ideal for applications that need to interact with other running processes or services, enabling data exchange and coordination.

TXMLConfig

Description:

A component for working with XML configuration files. It simplifies reading from and writing to XML files for application settings.

Usage:

Perfect for applications that store configuration or settings in XML format, offering a straightforward way to manage these settings.

TEventLog

Description:

A component for logging application events. It provides a simple interface for writing log entries to various targets.

Usage:

Useful in applications that need to maintain a log of events, errors, or other significant occurrences for debugging or auditing purposes.

The "System" tab in Lazarus focuses on components that provide functionalities related to system-level operations, such as running external processes, handling timers, managing inter-process communications, and logging. These components are crucial for developing applications that interact with the operating system, manage background tasks, or require communication with other processes. They offer the tools necessary to build more complex and feature-rich applications in Lazarus.

TSQLQuery

Description:

A component used to execute SQL queries on a database. It's designed to work with various SQL databases.

Usage:

Essential for applications that need to perform database operations like selecting, inserting, updating, or deleting data using SQL commands.

TSQLTransaction

Description:

Manages database transactions. It allows you to group several operations into a single transaction that can be committed or rolled back.

Usage:

Ideal for scenarios where multiple database operations must be treated as a single unit, ensuring data integrity and consistency, especially in complex database interactions.

TSQLConnector

Description:

Acts as a universal database connector, allowing you to connect to various database types (like MySQL, SQLite, PostgreSQL) without changing your code.

Usage:

Very useful for applications that need to interact with different types of databases, providing flexibility and ease of database management.

TSQLScript

Description:

Enables the execution of multiple SQL statements or scripts against a database. It can handle complex SQL scripts involving multiple commands.

Usage:

Perfect for initializing databases, performing batch operations, or executing complex SQL scripts as part of the application's workflow.

TSQLMonitor

Description:

A non-visual component for monitoring SQL commands sent to the database. It helps in debugging and optimizing database interactions.

Usage:

Beneficial for developers who need to track and analyze SQL queries and transactions for debugging, performance tuning, or auditing purposes.

The "SQLdb" tab in Lazarus is dedicated to components that facilitate interaction with SQL databases. These components are crucial for database-driven applications, providing the necessary tools for querying, transacting, connecting, scripting, and monitoring SQL databases.

They offer a powerful suite for developers to efficiently manage data in SQL-based applications, making database operations more streamlined and robust.

TColorButton

Description:

A button that displays a color and opens a color dialog when clicked. It's visually similar to a standard button but specifically designed for color selection.

Usage:

Ideal for applications that require users to select or change colors, such as graphic design tools, theme customizers, or any feature involving color customization.

TSpinEdit

Description:

An input control that allows users to adjust a numeric value using up and down spin buttons. It offers a convenient way to enter numeric values within a defined range.

Usage:

Useful for settings or configurations where users need to input numbers, like setting a timer, specifying dimensions, or adjusting quantities.

TFloatSpinEdit

Description:

Similar to TSpinEdit but for floating-point values. It allows users to input decimal numbers with the convenience of spin buttons.

Usage:

Perfect for applications requiring precise numerical input with decimals, such as financial tools, scientific calculators, or measurement adjustments.

TArrow

Description:

A simple graphical component used to display an arrow. It can be oriented in different directions and is purely for visual representation.

Usage:

Can be used in user interfaces to indicate direction, guide user navigation, or as a part of custom controls or indicators.

TCalendar

Description:

A visual calendar component that allows users to view and select dates. It displays a traditional month-view calendar.

Usage:

Essential for date selection in applications like scheduling tools, event planners, or any feature that requires users to pick a specific date.

TEditButton

Description:

Combines an editable text field with an attached button, allowing for custom actions to be associated with text input.

Usage:

Suitable for search bars, where the button can initiate a search, or for inputs that require an additional action, like browsing for a file.

TFileNameEdit

Description:

An enhanced edit box specifically for file path input, featuring an integrated button to open a file dialog.

Usage:

Great for applications that require users to select or input file paths, streamlining the process with a built-in file browser.

TDirectoryEdit

Description:

Similar to TFileNameEdit but for selecting directories. It includes a button to open a directory selection dialog.

Usage:

Ideal for settings or features where users need to specify a folder or directory, like setting a default save location or choosing a directory to scan.

TDateEdit

Description:

A specialized edit box for date input, equipped with a dropdown calendar for easy date selection.

Usage:

Perfect for forms, settings, or applications where date input is required, offering a user-friendly way to enter dates.

TCalcEdit

Description:

An edit control with an integrated button that opens a calculator dialog. Users can perform calculations and input the result directly.

Usage: Useful in financial or numerical applications where users might need to calculate values before entering them, like expense trackers or invoicing software.

TFileListBox

Description:

Displays a list of files from a specified directory. It's a convenient way to present file lists within the application.

Usage:

Suitable for file management features, allowing users to view and interact with files in a specific folder.

TXMLPropStorage

Description:

Provides functionality for storing and restoring various properties of your application, like window size or user preferences, in XML format.

Usage:

Ideal for applications that need to save settings between sessions, ensuring a consistent user experience.

TIniPropStorage

Description:

Similar to TXMLPropStorage but uses INI files for storing application properties. It's a simple and traditional way to handle configuration data.

Usage:

Useful for storing user settings, application state, or configuration parameters in a familiar INI file format.

TBarChart

Description:

A component for displaying bar charts, useful for visualizing data graphically.

Usage:

Great for applications that need to represent data in a bar chart format, like statistical tools, analytics dashboards, or reporting software.

TButtonPanel

Description:

Provides a panel with a predefined set of buttons like OK, Cancel, or Apply. It standardizes the button layout across the application.

Usage:

Ideal for dialog boxes or forms where standard action buttons are required, ensuring consistency in the user interface.

TIDEDialogLayoutStorage

Description:

A non-visual component that helps store and restore the layout of dialogs and windows in the Lazarus IDE.

Usage:

Mainly used by developers to maintain their preferred IDE layout, ensuring a personalized and efficient working environment.

The "Misc" tab in Lazarus offers a diverse range of utility components that enhance the functionality and aesthetics of user interfaces.

These components cater to specific needs like color selection, date input, file browsing, and data visualization, making them valuable for creating feature-rich and user-friendly applications.

TLazGroupBox

Description:

An enhanced version of the standard TGroupBox, providing additional customization and styling options. It's used for grouping related controls with a caption.

Usage:

Useful in forms and applications for organizing UI elements into logical sections, enhancing clarity and user experience.

TLazListView

Description:

An advanced version of the standard TListView, offering more features and flexibility. It displays items in a list format with various view options.

Usage:

Ideal for applications needing a robust list display, like file managers, data browsers, or settings panels.

TLazTreeView

Description:

An improved version of TTreeView, with added functionalities for displaying hierarchical data such as directories, categories, or organizational structures.

298

Usage:

Essential for applications that require a tree-based structure for navigation or data organization, like file explorers or hierarchical menus.

TLazVirtualTree

Description:

A highly customizable and efficient tree view that supports large data sets and virtualization. It dynamically loads data as needed.

Usage:

Best for applications dealing with extensive hierarchical data, where performance and flexibility are crucial, such as large databases or complex project structures.

TLazPageControl

Description:

A versatile container with multiple tabs, allowing users to switch between different views or sections within the same window.

Usage:

Great for organizing content into tabbed sections, like in settings dialogs, multi-section forms, or applications with modular interfaces.

TLazSynEdit

Description:

An advanced text editor component with syntax highlighting, code folding, and other features suitable for coding or text manipulation.

Usage:

Ideal for developing IDE-like applications, code editors, or any software requiring advanced text editing capabilities.

TLazTrayIcon

Description:

An enhanced system tray icon component that allows applications to minimize to the system tray and provide notifications or quick actions.

Usage:

Useful for background applications, system utilities, or any software that needs to provide quick access or notifications via the system tray.

TLazStringGrid

Description:

A powerful grid component for displaying and editing tabular data, offering extensive customization and interaction options.

Usage:

Perfect for applications that need to display data in a table format, like spreadsheets, database frontends, or data analysis tools.

TLazPanel

Description:

An extended panel component with additional features for layout
and design, used for grouping and organizing other controls.

Usage:

Effective in creating structured and visually appealing user
interfaces, particularly in complex forms or applications with
multiple UI elements.

TLazToolBar

Description:

A toolbar component that provides a convenient way to display a
set of tool buttons or actions, often used in conjunction with
menus.

Usage:

Essential for applications requiring quick access to tools or
commands, like graphic editors, word processors, or any
software with a rich feature set.

The "LazControls" tab in Lazarus is a collection of enhanced and
specialized components that offer additional functionalities over
the standard component set.

These components are designed to cater to more advanced
requirements in application development, providing developers
with tools to build sophisticated and feature-rich user interfaces.

TSynEdit

Description:

A powerful syntax highlighting text editor component designed for code editing. It supports multiple languages and customizable syntax schemes.

Usage:

Ideal for creating code editors, IDE-like applications, or any software that requires advanced text editing with syntax highlighting.

TSynAutoComplete

Description:

An add-on component for TSynEdit that provides automatic code completion functionality. It suggests possible completions based on the current context.

Usage:

Enhances user experience in code editors or IDEs by providing quick and relevant suggestions, making coding faster and more efficient.

TSynExporterHTML

Description:

A component that exports the contents of a TSynEdit editor to HTML format, preserving syntax highlighting and formatting.

Usage:

Useful for generating HTML documentation from code, sharing syntax-highlighted code snippets online, or for any application that needs to convert code to HTML.

TSynMacroRecorder

Description:

Allows recording and playback of keystrokes and actions in a TSynEdit editor, automating repetitive tasks.

Usage:

Adds macro recording capabilities to text editors or IDEs, helping users automate repetitive editing tasks and improve efficiency.

TSynMemo

Description:

A memo component based on TSynEdit, providing advanced text editing with syntax highlighting, but simpler than the full

TSynEdit.

Usage:

Suitable for applications that require a multi-line text editor with advanced features but don't need the full power of TSynEdit.

TSynPasSyn

Description:

A syntax highlighter for Pascal language, specifically designed for use with TSynEdit.

Usage: Perfect for Pascal code editors or IDEs, highlighting Pascal syntax to improve readability and code understanding.

TSynFreePascalSyn

Description:

A syntax highlighter tailored for Free Pascal, offering specific highlighting rules for Free Pascal language constructs.

Usage:

Ideal for Free Pascal development environments or editors, providing syntax highlighting that aligns with Free Pascal's language features.

TSynCppSyn

Description:

A C++ syntax highlighter for TSynEdit, highlighting C++ language syntax elements.

Usage:

Enhances C++ code editors or IDEs by visually distinguishing syntax elements, making C++ code more readable and manageable.

TSynJavaSyn

Description:

Provides syntax highlighting for Java language in TSynEdit components.

Usage:

Useful in Java code editors, IDEs, or any application where Java code needs to be edited with syntax highlighting.

TSynPerlSyn

Description:

A Perl syntax highlighter for TSynEdit, designed to highlight Perl language constructs.

Usage:

Essential for Perl scripting editors or tools where Perl code needs to be displayed with clear syntax differentiation.

TSynHTMLSyn

Description:

Offers syntax highlighting for HTML, making it easier to edit web pages or HTML documents in a TSynEdit component.

Usage:

Ideal for web development tools, HTML editors, or any software dealing with HTML content editing.

TSynXMLSyn

Description:

Provides syntax highlighting for XML files in TSynEdit, enhancing the readability and editing of XML documents.

Usage:

Perfect for applications that involve XML editing or management, such as configuration tools, data processing applications, or web services development.

TSynLFMSyn

Description:

A syntax highlighter for Lazarus Form files (LFM), integrating with TSynEdit to highlight LFM content.

Usage:

Useful for Lazarus development, allowing developers to edit and manage LFM files with enhanced visibility of form properties and structures.

TSynUNIXShellScriptSyn

Description:

Highlights UNIX shell script syntax in TSynEdit, aiding in the creation or editing of shell scripts.

Usage:

Ideal for scripting tools, UNIX/Linux development environments, or applications that involve shell script editing.

TSynCssSyn

Description:

A CSS (Cascading Style Sheets) syntax highlighter for TSynEdit, making it easier to write and edit CSS code.

Usage:

Essential for web designers and developers working on styling web pages, providing a clear view of CSS code structure.

TSynPHPSyn

Description:

Highlights PHP scripting language syntax in TSynEdit components.

Usage:

Enhances PHP development environments or editors by providing syntax highlighting, aiding in the readability and management of PHP scripts.

TSynTeXSyn

Description:

A syntax highlighter for TeX/LaTeX documents, integrating with TSynEdit for editing scientific and technical documents.

Usage:

Ideal for academic, scientific, or technical writing software where TeX/LaTeX is used for document formatting and typesetting.

TSynSQLSyn

Description:

Highlights SQL query syntax in TSynEdit, aiding in writing and managing SQL queries and database scripts.

Usage:

Useful for database management tools, SQL query editors, or any application that involves writing or editing SQL code.

TSynPythonSyn

Description:

A Python syntax highlighter for TSynEdit, designed to enhance Python code editing and readability.

Usage:

Perfect for Python development tools, script editors, or any software that requires editing Python scripts with syntax highlighting.

TSynVBSyn

Description:

Provides syntax highlighting for Visual Basic Script (VBScript) in TSynEdit.

Usage:

Ideal for applications that involve VBScript editing, such as automation tools, scripting environments, or web development.

TSynAnySyn

Description:

A generic syntax highlighter that can be customized for different languages in TSynEdit.

Usage:

Offers flexibility for developing custom code editors or IDEs where specific or unusual language syntax needs to be highlighted.

TSynMultiSyn

Description:

Allows combining multiple syntax highlighters in a single TSynEdit component, useful for files containing mixed code.

Usage:

Essential for editors or IDEs dealing with files that include multiple programming languages or syntax types, such as web files with HTML, CSS, and JavaScript.

The "SynEdit" tab in Lazarus is a collection of components and tools specifically designed for advanced text and code editing.

These components offer a wide range of functionalities for syntax highlighting, code editing, and formatting, catering to various programming languages and text editing requirements.

They are particularly useful for developing specialized text editors, IDEs, and tools for software development and scripting.

TCollectionPropertyEditor

Description:

An editor component for managing collections at design time. It allows you to edit properties of items in a collection, such as a list of objects.

Usage:

Useful in scenarios where you need to customize and manage a collection of objects or components in your application, providing an intuitive interface for setting properties.

TSetPropertyEditor

Description:

A property editor designed to handle and edit set properties. Sets in Pascal are collections of values of a particular type.

Usage:

Ideal for applications that utilize set types for managing groups of elements or properties, offering an easy way to edit these sets in the Lazarus environment.

TClassPropertyEditor

Description:

An editor for properties of type TClass. It provides a user interface for selecting and modifying class properties in design time.

Usage:

Beneficial for applications that rely on class-based configurations or settings, enabling developers to visually manage class properties within the Lazarus IDE.

TComponentPropertyEditor

Description:

A dedicated property editor for components. It allows for the selection and configuration of component properties in a user-friendly way.

Usage:

Essential for applications with complex component structures, simplifying the task of setting up and configuring various component properties.

TMethodPropertyEditor

Description:

Designed for editing method properties, this editor simplifies the process of assigning event handlers and methods to component events.

Usage:

Perfect for setting up event-driven functionalities in your application, streamlining the process of linking events to their corresponding methods.

TCollectionItemPropertyEditor

Description:

Focuses on editing properties of individual items within a collection. It's tailored for detailed customization of collection items.

Usage:

Useful when you need to fine-tune the properties of items in a collection, such as a list of controls or objects, enhancing the control over collection elements.

TInterfacePropertyEditor

Description:

An editor designed for properties that implement interfaces. It aids in managing and setting up interface-based properties.

Usage:

Ideal for applications using interface-oriented programming, providing a straightforward way to configure and manage interface properties.

TIDPropertyEditor

Description:

Simplifies editing of properties that are identifiers or IDs. This editor is tailored to handle unique identifiers or reference properties.

Usage:

Beneficial in scenarios where managing unique identifiers or references is crucial, such as in database applications or complex data structures.

TEnumPropertyEditor

Description:

A property editor specifically for enumeration types. It provides a drop-down list for selecting enumeration values.

Usage:

Essential for properties that are of an enumerated type, offering an easy and error-free way of selecting enumeration values.

The RTTI (Run-Time Type Information) tab in Lazarus contains a collection of specialized property editors designed to enhance the design-time experience in the Lazarus IDE.

These components are particularly useful for developers who need advanced capabilities in editing and configuring various property types, such as collections, sets, classes, methods, and more.

They provide a more intuitive and efficient way to handle complex property configurations, making them invaluable tools in the development of sophisticated Lazarus applications.

TIpHtmlPanel

Description:

A panel component designed to display HTML content. It renders HTML and can handle basic formatting and hyperlinks.

Usage:

Ideal for applications that need to display formatted text or web content within the application interface, such as help pages or simple web pages.

TIpHtmlDataProvider

Description:

A provider component that supplies HTML content to other IPro components like TIpHtmlPanel. It manages the retrieval and supply of HTML data.

Usage:

Useful in scenarios where dynamic HTML content needs to be displayed, fetched from various sources or dynamically generated.

TIpFileDataProvider

Description:

A specialized data provider that fetches HTML content from files. It extends TIpHtmlDataProvider to handle file-based HTML data.

Usage:

Perfect for applications that display HTML content stored in local files, such as offline documentation or file-based help systems.

TIpHttpDataProvider

Description:

This component retrieves HTML content over HTTP, making it possible to display web pages or online content in a Lazarus application.

Usage: Essential for applications that need to integrate online content, such as displaying web pages or fetching online HTML data.

TIpHtml

Description:

The core HTML rendering component in the IPro tab. It's responsible for parsing and rendering HTML content.

Usage:

The backbone for any application feature that requires HTML rendering, such as custom web browsers or HTML viewers.

The IPro tab in Lazarus focuses on components that are useful for handling and displaying HTML content.

These components are particularly beneficial for developers creating applications that need to integrate web content or display HTML in a user-friendly manner.

Whether it's fetching HTML data from local files, online sources, or simply rendering HTML content within the application, the IPro tab offers a range of components to facilitate these functionalities.

This makes it easier for developers to incorporate web technologies into their Lazarus applications, enhancing the versatility and capability of their software.

TChart

Description:

A versatile chart component that serves as the base for creating different types of charts. It provides a variety of customization options to tailor the appearance and behavior of the chart.

Usage:

Ideal for any application that needs to represent data graphically, such as in business analytics, scientific data visualization, or statistical representation.

TBarSeries

Description:

A chart series component for creating bar charts. It allows for the representation of data in the form of vertical or horizontal bars.

Usage:

Best suited for comparing different groups of data visually, often used in financial analysis, inventory management, or survey results.

TLineSeries

Description:

This component is used to create line charts, connecting individual data points with lines. It's effective for showing trends or changes over time.

Usage:

Commonly used in applications that track changes over periods, like stock market trends, temperature changes, or performance metrics.

TPieSeries

Description:

A component for creating pie charts, which are circular statistical graphics divided into slices to illustrate numerical proportions.

Usage:

Essential for displaying proportions or percentages in various fields, such as market share analysis, budget allocations, or demographic studies.

TAreaSeries

Description:

Used to create area charts, which are similar to line charts but with the area below the line filled with color. It highlights the magnitude of change over time.

Usage:

Useful for emphasizing the degree of change, often seen in environmental data representation, resource usage, or cumulative data analysis.

TPointSeries

Description:

Designed for plotting individual data points on a chart without connecting them with lines. Each point is represented as a dot or similar marker.

Usage: Great for scatter plots to show the distribution or relationship between two variables, used in scientific research, quality control, or statistical analysis.

TChartListbox

Description:

A listbox component that integrates with TChart to provide a user interface for selecting and managing different chart series.

Usage:

Enhances the interactivity of charts by allowing users to select which data series to view, hide, or customize, making it user-friendly for applications with complex data sets.

The Chart tab in Lazarus is a powerful toolset for developers who need to incorporate data visualization into their applications. It offers a range of components for constructing various chart types, each with its specific use case.

These chart components can transform raw data into meaningful visual insights, making them invaluable in applications where data analysis and reporting are key features.

Whether it's for business intelligence, scientific research, or any domain where data visualization is crucial, the Chart tab provides the necessary tools to create compelling and informative charts.

TPSScript:

Description:

The primary component for implementing Pascal scripting functionality. It acts as a container and interpreter for Pascal scripts.

Usage:

Used to add script execution capabilities to applications, allowing users to execute custom scripts written in a Pascal-like language. It's ideal for applications requiring customizable or user-generated scripts.

TPSEvents:

Description:

A component that provides event handling capabilities for scripts executed by TPSScript.

Usage:

Essential for applications where scripts need to respond to or trigger events, such as button clicks, timer events, or other interactive elements.

TPSImport_Classes:

Description:

Provides access to common classes and routines in Pascal scripts, allowing scripts to use standard classes like TStringList, TObjectList, etc.

Usage:

Ideal for scripts that require the use of common Pascal classes, enhancing the script's functionality and integration with the main application.

TPSImport_DateUtils:

Description:

Enables the use of date and time utilities in scripts, such as date calculations, formatting, and conversions.

Usage:

Useful for applications where scripts need to handle date and time operations, like scheduling, logging, or time-based calculations.

TPSImport_DB:

Description:

Allows scripts to interact with databases, providing access to database components and functionality.

Usage:

Used in applications where scripts need to perform database operations, such as querying, updating, or managing data.

TPSImport_Forms:

Description:

Gives scripts access to form-related classes and properties, enabling the manipulation of forms and controls at runtime.

Usage:

Essential for scripts that need to create, modify, or interact with forms and their components, adding a dynamic layer to the user interface.

TPSCompilerMessages:

Description:

A component that captures and displays messages generated during the compilation of scripts, such as errors or warnings.

Usage:

Helpful for debugging scripts by providing detailed feedback on script compilation issues, assisting in the development and troubleshooting of scripts.

By leveraging these components, developers can greatly enhance the flexibility and capabilities of their Lazarus applications, allowing for dynamic and customizable scripting solutions that can adapt to a wide range of use cases and user requirements.

Each object has different properties and events. In this case, I have selected Form1's major properties and events.

OBJECT INSPECTOR : PROPERTIES

Align:

Determines how the form is aligned within its parent container.

AllowDropFiles:

Enables the form to accept files that are dragged and dropped onto it.

AlphaBlend:

Enables the use of alpha blending, making the form partially transparent.

AlphaBlendValue:

Specifies the degree of transparency applied to the form when AlphaBlend is true.

Anchors:

Determines how the form is anchored to its parent, allowing it to maintain its position relative to the edges of the parent.

AutoScroll:

Enables automatic scrolling for the form when its contents exceed the visible area.

AutoSize:

Automatically adjusts the size of the form to fit its contents.

BiDiMode:

Specifies the bidirectional mode for the form, used for languages that read right-to-left.

BorderIcons:

Specifies the icons which appear in the title bar for the form.

BorderStyle:

The border style affects the title bar, border and resize behavior of the form.

BorderWidth:

Width of the Border around the control; default is zero.

Caption:

The text that appears in the title bar of the form.

Color:

Sets the background color of the form.

Cursor: Determines the type of cursor displayed when the mouse pointer is over the form.

DesignTimePPI:

Design-time Pixels Per Inch for the designer surface. Default is 96.

DoubleBuffered:

Reduces flickering by drawing to an off-screen buffer before displaying on the screen.

DragKind:

Specifies the type of drag operation the form supports.

DragMode:

Determines how drag-and-drop operations are initiated.

Enabled:

Determines whether the form can respond to user input.

Font:

Defines the default font for controls on the form.

FontStyle:

Specifies the style of the font used in the form.

Height:

The height of the form.

HelpContext:

The context ID for the form's Help topic.

HelpFile:

The name of the Help file associated with the form.

HelpKeyword:

A keyword for invoking Help.

HelpType:

Specifies the type of Help provided (keyword, context).

Hint:

A string that provides additional information about the form, typically displayed as a tooltip.

HorzScrollBar:

Properties of the form's horizontal scrollbar.

Icon:

The icon displayed in the form's title bar and taskbar.

KeyPreview:

Allows the form to receive key events before they are passed to the focused control.

Left:

The horizontal coordinate of the form's top-left corner relative to its parent.

Menu:

Associates a main menu with the form.

Name:

The name of the form, used as an identifier in code.

ParentFont:

Inherits the font settings from the parent control.

PixelsPerInch:

The resolution of the form in pixels per inch.

PopupParent:

Specifies the parent form for a popup form.

Position:

Determines how the form is positioned when shown (centered, manual, etc.).

Scaled:

Determines whether the form scales its contents based on the screen resolution.

ShowHint:

Controls whether hints are shown for controls on the form.

ShowInTaskBar:

Determines whether the form appears in the Windows taskbar.

Tag:

An integer value associated with the form for use in code.

Top:

The vertical coordinate of the form's top-left corner relative to its parent.

VertScrollBar:

Properties of the form's vertical scrollbar.

Visible:

Controls the visibility of the form.

Width:

The width of the form.

WindowState:

Controls how the form is displayed (normal, minimized, maximized).

OnActivate:

Triggered when a form becomes active.

OnCanResize:

Allows dynamic control over the resizing of a component.

OnChange:

Triggered when the value of a control changes.

OnClick:

Occurs when a control is clicked.

OnCloseQuery:

Occurs before a form or application closes, allowing cancellation of the close.

OnConstrainedResize:

Provides constraints to the resizing of a component.

OnContextPopup:

Triggered when a context menu is requested on a control.

OnCreate:

Triggered when a form or other component is created.

OnDblClick:

Triggered when a control is double-clicked.

OnDeactivate:

Occurs when a form becomes inactive.

OnDestroy:

Occurs when a form or component is about to be destroyed.

OnDockDrop:

Triggered during docking when a dragged control is dropped.

OnDockOver:

Occurs when a dragged control is over a potential docking target.

OnDragDrop:

Triggered during a drag-and-drop operation when an object is dropped onto a control.

OnDragOver:

Occurs when an object is dragged over a control.

OnEndDock:

Triggered when a docking operation ends.

OnEndDrag:

Triggered when a drag-and-drop operation ends.

OnEnter:

Occurs when a control gains focus.

OnExit:

Triggered when a control loses focus.

OnGetSiteInfo:

Provides information about a control's docking site.

OnHide:

Occurs when a control becomes invisible.

OnKeyDown:

Occurs when a key is pressed while the control has focus.

OnKeyPress:

Triggered when a key is pressed and released over a control.

OnKeyUp:

Occurs when a key is released while the control has focus.

OnMouseDown:

Triggered when the mouse button is pressed down over a control.

OnMouseEnter:

Occurs when the mouse enters a control.

OnMouseLeave:

Triggered when the mouse leaves a control.

OnMouseMove:

Occurs when the mouse is moved over a control.

OnMouseUp:

Triggered when the mouse button is released over a control.

OnMouseWheel:

Occurs when the mouse wheel is rotated over a control.

OnMouseWheelDown:

Triggered when the mouse wheel is scrolled down over a component.

OnMouseWheelUp:

Occurs when the mouse wheel is scrolled up over a component.

OnPaint:

Occurs when a control needs to be repainted.

OnResize:

Triggered when a control is resized.

OnShow:

Triggered when a control becomes visible.

OnStartDock:

Occurs when a docking operation starts.

OnStartDrag:

Occurs when a drag-and-drop operation starts.

OnUnDock:

Triggered when a control is undocked.

Mathematical Functions

Functions in this category deal with mathematical operations and are essential for calculations in various types of programs.

Sin(x):

Returns: The sine of x, where x is in radians.
Example: Result := Sin(PI / 2); // Result is 1

Cos(x):

Returns: The cosine of x, where x is in radians.
Example: Result := Cos(PI); // Result is -1

*** there is no tan(x). However, you can calculate the value like below:
    tan(x) := sin(x) / cos(x)

Sqrt(x):

Returns: The square root of x.
Example: Result := Sqrt(9); // Result is 3
Power(x, y):

Returns: x raised to the power of y.
Example: Result := Power(2, 3); // Result is 8

Abs(x):

Description: Returns the absolute value of x.
Example Usage: Result := Abs(-5); // Result is 5

Exp(x):

Description: Returns the value of e (the base of natural logarithms) raised to the power of x.
Example Usage: Result := Exp(2); // Result is approximately 7.389

Ln(x):

Description: Returns the natural logarithm of x.
Example Usage: Result := Ln(7.389); // Result is approximately2

Log10(x):

Description: Returns the base-10 logarithm of x.
Example Usage: Result := Log10(100); // Result is 2

Round(x):

Description: Rounds the floating-point value x to the nearest integer.
Example Usage: Result := Round(3.6); // Result is 4

Trunc(x):

Description: Truncates the floating-point value x to an integer.
Example Usage: Result := Trunc(3.9); // Result is 3
Frac(x):

Description: Returns the fractional part of the floating-point number x.
Example Usage: Result := Frac(5.75); // Result is 0.75

Mod(x, y):

Description: Returns the remainder of x divided by y.
Example Usage: Result := Mod(17, 5); // Result is 2

RandomRange(Low, High):

Description: Returns a random integer between Low and High
(inclusive).
Example Usage: Result := RandomRange(10, 20); // Result is a
random number between 10 and 20

Ceil(x):

Description: Returns the smallest integer that is greater than or
equal to x.
Example Usage: Result := Ceil(3.2); // Result is 4

Floor(x):

Description: Returns the largest integer that is less than or equal
to x.
Example Usage: Result := Floor(3.8); // Result is 3

ArcSin(x):

Description: Returns the arcsine (in radians) of x.
Example Usage: Result := ArcSin(1); // Result is PI/2

ArcCos(x):

Description: Returns the arccosine (in radians) of x.
Example Usage: Result := ArcCos(0); // Result is PI/2

ArcTan(x):

Description: Returns the arctangent (in radians) of x.
Example Usage: Result := ArcTan(1); // Result is PI/4
ArcTan2(y, x):

Description: Returns the arctangent (in radians) of y/x, taking
into account the signs of both to determine the quadrant.
Example Usage: Result := ArcTan2(1, 1); // Result is PI/4

Hypot(x, y):

Description: Returns the square root of the sum of squares of x
and y, i.e., sqrt(x*x + y*y). Useful for calculating the length of
the hypotenuse of a right-angled triangle.
Example Usage: Result := Hypot(3, 4); // Result is 5

String Manipulation Functions

These functions handle operations on strings, such as searching,
replacing, or modifying string content.

Length(s):

Returns: The length of the string s.
Example: Result := Length('Hello'); // Result is 5

Pos(substr, str):

Returns: The position of substring substr in string str.
Example: Result := Pos('World', 'Hello World'); // Result is 7

Copy(s, start, len):

Returns: A substring of s starting from start for len characters.
Example: Result := Copy('Hello', 2, 3); // Result is 'ell'

Concat(s1, s2, ...):

Returns: A concatenation of the strings s1, s2, etc.
Example: Result := Concat('Hello', ' ', 'World'); // Result is 'Hello World'

Date and Time Functions

Functions for handling and manipulating dates and times.

Now:

Returns: The current date and time.
Example: Result := Now; // Result is the current date and time
Date:

Returns: The current date.
Example: Result := Date; // Result is the current date

Time:

Returns: The current time.
Example: Result := Time; // Result is the current time
EncodeDate(Year, Month, Day):

Returns: A TDateTime value for a given year, month, and day.
Example: Result := EncodeDate(2021, 12, 31); // Result is the TDateTime of 31st Dec 2021
Conversion Functions

Functions convert data from one type to another.

IntToStr(i):

Returns: The integer i as a string.
Example: Result := IntToStr(100); // Result is '100'

StrToInt(s):

Returns: The string s as an integer.
Example: Result := StrToInt('100'); // Result is 100

FloatToStr(f):

Returns: The floating-point number f as a string.
Example: Result := FloatToStr(3.14); // Result is '3.14'

StrToFloat(s):

Returns: The string s as a floating-point number.
Example: Result := StrToFloat('3.14'); // Result is 3.14

File and Directory Functions

Functions for working with files and directories.

FileExists(filename):

Returns: True if the file filename exists.
Example: Result := FileExists('myfile.txt');

DirectoryExists(dir):

Returns: True if the directory dir exists.
Example: Result := DirectoryExists('myfolder');

CreateDir(dir):

Effect: Creates a new directory dir.
Example: Result := CreateDir('newfolder');

AssignFile(var F: File; filename: string):

Role: Assigns the file name filename to the file variable F. This allows you to perform file read and write operations using F.

Reset(F: File):

Role: Opens the file F in read mode. It is used before performing any file reading operations.

Rewrite(F: File):

Role: Opens the file F in write mode. It creates a new file and overwrites an existing file if it exists.

Append(F: File):

Role: Opens the file F in write mode, but instead of overwriting an existing file, it appends data to the end of the file.

CloseFile(F: File):

Role: Closes the file F. It should always be called after file reading or writing operations are completed.

FilePos(F: File):

Role: Returns the current position within the file F in bytes.

FileSize(F: File):

Role: Returns the size of the file F in bytes.

EOF(F: File):

Role: The EOF(F) function checks whether the end-of-file condition has been reached while reading from the file F. It returns True if the end of the file has been reached, indicating that there is no more data to read.

In Lazarus and Pascal programming, the uses clause is an essential part of the language.

It serves to include external units (libraries or modules) into your current program or unit.

This inclusion allows your code to access and use the functions, procedures, classes, and types defined in these external units.

Let's break down the example you provided and explain each part:

Example:

```
uses
    Classes, SysUtils, Forms, Controls, Graphics, ExtCtrls, Math;
```

Explanation:

Classes:

This unit contains core classes that are essential for Lazarus and Delphi applications. It includes definitions for fundamental classes like TComponent, TStream, and many others that form the base for component-based development.

SysUtils:

The System Utilities unit. It provides a wide range of functions and classes for various purposes, like file handling, string manipulation, date and time functions, and more. It's one of the most frequently used units as it contains essential utilities for everyday programming tasks.

Forms:

This unit is central to Lazarus and Delphi's form-based application development. It includes the TForm class, which is the base class for all form objects – the windows or dialogs in a GUI application.

Controls:

This unit contains the base classes for all visual control components. Classes in this unit provide basic functionality for input, display, and control elements in the GUI, such as buttons, edit boxes, and labels.

Graphics:

As the name suggests, this unit deals with graphical elements. It provides classes and routines for drawing, painting, and handling images and graphical objects.

ExtCtrls:

Short for "Extended Controls", this unit includes additional GUI control components that are more specialized or advanced than those found in the Controls unit. Examples include panels, static text, image components, and shape components.

Math:

This unit provides mathematical functions and routines. It includes a range of mathematical operations and types, particularly useful for complex calculations or scientific applications.

** When you use math function, you need to add **Math** manually in uses.

** When you use virtual keyboard, you need to add **LCLType** manually in uses.

** When you use dialog, you need to add **Dialogs** manually in uses.

Importance of the uses Clause:

Modularity:

It promotes modular programming by allowing you to use only the parts of the library that are needed for your application, keeping the program efficient and reducing its size.

Code Reuse:

Enables the reuse of code, as units often contain reusable classes and procedures.

Functionality Extension:

By using different units, you can extend the functionality of your program without having to write all the code from scratch.

In Lazarus, when you create a new form or project, the IDE automatically adds a default set of units to the uses clause, which are commonly needed for typical applications.

This automation makes it easier for beginners, as they don't need to know all the necessary units from the start.

However, understanding what each unit does is crucial as you progress and start building more complex applications.

Classes:

Core classes for component-based applications, like TComponent and TStream.

SysUtils:

System utilities for file handling, string manipulation, date and time functions.

Forms:

Base unit for form-based applications, includes the TForm class.

Controls:

Contains base classes for GUI control components.

Graphics:

For drawing, painting, and handling images and graphical objects.

ExtCtrls:

Extended GUI control components, like panels and image components.

Math:

Provides mathematical functions and routines.

Dialogs:

Contains classes and functions for standard dialog boxes.

345

StdCtrls:

Standard GUI control components like buttons, edit boxes, and labels.

ComCtrls:

Common GUI control components like tabs, toolbars, and status bars.

Menus:

For creating and managing menus in applications.

ActnList:

For managing actions in an application, useful for menus and toolbars.

LCLType:

Defines basic LCL types, constants, and classes.

LCLIntf:

Interface unit for the LCL, providing cross-platform features.

LCLProc:

Contains LCL-specific procedures and functions.

DateUtils:

For handling and manipulating dates and times.

FileUtil:

Helper functions for file operations.

StrUtils:

Additional string manipulation functions.

Types:

Defines basic types and utility functions.

Variants:

Support for variant types.

DB:

Base unit for database-related components.

FMTBcd:

For handling BCD (Binary Coded Decimal) fields in databases.

SQLDB:

For working with SQL databases in Lazarus.

XMLRead:

For reading XML documents.

XMLWrite:

For writing XML documents.

Each unit in this list provides a set of functionalities, ranging from GUI components to database handling, file operations, and more.

When writing a Lazarus application, you include the units that contain the functionalities or components you need.

This approach promotes modular programming, allowing you to pick and choose the specific capabilities required for your application.

Backup the Project Folder

Why?

Safety Net:

Backups act as a safety net. If you accidentally overwrite or delete something important, you can restore it from the backup.

Protection Against Data Loss:

Various issues, such as software crashes or hardware failures, can lead to data loss. Regular backups minimize this risk.

How to Solve:

Manual Backup:

Regularly copy your entire project folder to a different location on your computer or an external drive.

Automated Tools:

Use software that automatically backs up files at set intervals.

Frequent Compile

Why?

Early Error Detection:

Compiling frequently helps you catch syntax and logical errors early in the development process.

Consistent Code Quality:

Regular checks ensure that your code remains clean and free from accumulating errors.

How to Solve:

Compile Habit:

Make it a habit to compile your code after writing a significant amount of code or completing a functional part.

Leave Comments in Code

Why?

Clarity for Future Self:

Your future self may not remember your current thought process. Comments can save hours of re-figuring out what your code does.

Helps Others Understand:

If someone else needs to read or use your code, comments will be invaluable.

How to Solve:

Comment as You Code:

Add comments while you're writing the code, not afterwards. It's much easier and more effective.

Use Memo1 for Monitoring Variables

Why?

Visual Feedback:

Seeing the values of variables change in real time can be incredibly helpful for understanding how your code behaves.

Debugging Aid:

It's a simple yet powerful way to track down where things might be going wrong in your code.

How to Solve:

Print to Memo:

Use Memo1.Append() to display variable values and other information during runtime.

Visibility Toggle:

Set Memo1.Visible to false when you don't need this feature for a cleaner interface.

Manage Program Versions in Comments

Why?

Track Changes:

Knowing which version of the program has certain features or bugs is crucial for effective development and maintenance.

User Communication:

Helps communicate changes and updates to users effectively.

How to Solve:

Version Commenting:

Include a comment at the top of your main program file indicating the version number and change log.

Keyboard Blind Touch Techniques

Why?

Efficiency:

The faster and more accurately you can type, the more efficiently you can code.

Focus on Logic, Not Typing:

Proficient typing allows you to concentrate more on problem-solving and less on the act of typing.

How to Solve:

Practice:

Regular practice is key. Use typing games and exercises to improve your speed and accuracy.

Consistent Layout:

Stick to one keyboard layout to build muscle memory.

Lazarus(PASCAL) is Object Oriented Pascal.
In general, OOP, however, is hard to understand. In this section,
First I show you some sample of OOP code. Then at the end, I
am going to state what is OOP.

INTRODUCTION TO OOP IN LAZARUS PASCAL USING FORM1

Familiarity with Form1:

In Lazarus, when you create a new project, you typically start
with a Form (usually named Form1). This Form1 is actually an
instance of a class. Without realizing it, you're already stepping
into the world of OOP.

Form1 as an Object:

In Lazarus, Form1 is an object. It's an instance of the TForm
class, which is predefined in Lazarus. When you're designing
your Form1, you're actually working with an object.

Properties and Events:

The properties you set in the Object Inspector (like size, color,
caption) are part of OOP. These properties are variables defined
in the TForm class.

353

Events like OnClick, OnCreate, etc., are methods associated with the TForm class. When you write code for these events, you're actually writing methods.

Understanding OOP Through Form1:

Class and Object: TForm is a class. Form1 is an object of this class. When you create a new form, you're creating a new object.

Encapsulation:

The properties and methods (events) of Form1 are encapsulated within the TForm class. You interact with them through the Object Inspector and the Lazarus code editor.

Inheritance: TForm inherits from TWinControl, which inherits from TControl, and so on. This means Form1 has properties and methods from all these parent classes.

Practical Example:

Adding a Button to Form1

Let's consider a simple example of adding a button to Form1 and writing an OnClick event.

Adding a Button:

When you drop a TButton onto Form1, you're creating an instance of the TButton class (an object).

Setting Properties: You set properties like Caption, Size, and Position in the Object Inspector. These are predefined in the TButton class.

Writing an OnClick Event:

When you write code for the button's OnClick event, you're defining what should happen when the button (object) is clicked.

```
procedure TForm1.Button1Click(Sender: TObject);
begin
  ShowMessage('Button clicked!');
end;
```

In this code, Button1Click is a method associated with Form1 (TForm object), responding to an event of the Button1 (TButton object).

Conclusion

OOP in Lazarus Pascal is not as intimidating as it might seem. If you've used Form1, set properties, and written event handlers, you've already been using OOP principles. Understanding these concepts can make your journey into more advanced OOP smoother and more intuitive. By recognizing these patterns in familiar Lazarus components, you can gradually build a solid foundation in OOP.

```
unit Unit1;

{$mode objfpc}{$H+}

interface

uses
  Classes, SysUtils, Forms, Controls, Graphics, Dialogs,
StdCtrls;

type
  // TForm1 is a subclass of TForm
  TForm1 = class(TForm)
    Button1: TButton;
    Memo1: TMemo;
    procedure Button1Click(Sender: TObject);
  private
    // Private members are accessible only within this class
    FMessage: String;
    procedure ShowMessageInMemo;
  public
    // Public members can be accessed from outside this class
    constructor Create(TheOwner: TComponent); override;
  end;

var
  Form1: TForm1;

implementation

{$R *.lfm}

{ TForm1 }

// Constructor for TForm1
constructor TForm1.Create(TheOwner: TComponent);
begin
  inherited Create(TheOwner);
  FMessage := 'Hello World!';
end;
```

```
// Event handler for Button1's click event
procedure TForm1.Button1Click(Sender: TObject);
begin
  ShowMessageInMemo;
end;

// Private method to display a message in Memo1
procedure TForm1.ShowMessageInMemo;
begin
  Memo1.Lines.Text := FMessage;
end;

end.
```

OOP Concepts Illustrated in the Example

Class and Object:

TForm1 is a class derived from the TForm class. It represents the form of the application.
Form1 is an object, an instance of the TForm1 class.

Inheritance:

TForm1 inherits properties and methods from its parent class TForm. This includes components like Memo1 and Button1.

Encapsulation:

The FMessage string is a private member of TForm1. It's encapsulated within the class and not directly accessible from outside.
ShowMessageInMemo is a private method, meaning it can only be called within the TForm1 class.

357

Public Interface:

The constructor Create and the event handler Button1Click are public. They can be accessed and used by other parts of the application or other units.

Event Handling:

Button1Click is an event handler method linked to the OnClick event of Button1. When the button is clicked, this method is executed.

Scope of Private and Public Data:

Private data, like FMessage, is used to maintain the internal state of the class. It's a way to hide the internal workings of the class from the outside world.
Public methods provide a controlled way to interact with the class. They form the class's interface with the rest of the application.

Enhanced TBankAccount Class

```
type
  TBankAccount = class
  private
    AccountNumber: String;
    Balance: Double;
    CustomerName: String;
    CustomerAddress: String;
  public
    constructor Create(const Name, Address: String; const
InitialBalance: Double);
    procedure Deposit(const Amount: Double);
    procedure Withdraw(const Amount: Double);
    function GetCurrentBalance: Double;
  end;

constructor TBankAccount.Create(const Name, Address:
String; const InitialBalance: Double);
begin
  CustomerName := Name;
  CustomerAddress := Address;
  Balance := InitialBalance;
end;

procedure TBankAccount.Deposit(const Amount: Double);
begin
  if Amount > 0 then
    Balance := Balance + Amount;
end;

procedure TBankAccount.Withdraw(const Amount: Double);
begin
  if (Amount > 0) and (Amount <= Balance) then
    Balance := Balance - Amount;
end;

function TBankAccount.GetCurrentBalance: Double;
begin
  Result := Balance;
end;
```

Using the TBankAccount Class

Scenario:

First, Creating bank account:

Wolfy , Now York , $400
Mary , California , $1,000

Second, Transactions:

Wolfy deposits $300
Mary wisdraws $100

```
var
   WolfysAccount, MarysAccount: TBankAccount;
begin
   // Creating accounts
   WolfysAccount := TBankAccount.Create('Wolfy', 'New York',
400);
   MarysAccount := TBankAccount.Create('Mary', 'California',
1000);

   // Wolfy deposits $300, new balance should be $700
   WolfysAccount.Deposit(300);
   WriteLn('Wolfy''s new balance: $',
WolfysAccount.GetCurrentBalance:0:2);

   // Mary withdraws $100, new balance should be $900
   MarysAccount.Withdraw(100);
   WriteLn('Mary''s new balance: $',
MarysAccount.GetCurrentBalance:0:2);

   // ... other operations ...

   // Freeing the objects
   WolfysAccount.Free;
   MarysAccount.Free;
end;
```

OOP Concepts in the TBankAccount Class

1. Class Definition

TBankAccount is a class that represents a bank account. It's a blueprint for creating bank account objects with specific attributes and behaviors.

2. Encapsulation

Private Members: AccountNumber, Balance, CustomerName, and CustomerAddress are private fields. They are encapsulated within the class, meaning they can't be accessed directly from outside the class. This encapsulation ensures data integrity and security.

3. Constructor

Create Method: This is the constructor of the TBankAccount class. It initializes new instances of the class with specific values. When you create a new bank account object, this method sets up the initial state of that object (name, address, and balance).

4. Methods (Behaviors)

Deposit and Withdraw: These are public methods that allow interaction with the bank account object. They modify the Balance based on transactions, adhering to business rules (e.g., no withdrawal beyond the current balance).

GetCurrentBalance:

This function provides a safe way to access the private Balance field. It's a read-only access, ensuring the balance can't be modified unexpectedly.

Using the TBankAccount Class

Scenario:

Managing Bank Accounts for Wolfy and Mary

Creating Accounts:

WolfysAccount and MarysAccount are objects of the TBankAccount class. They are created using the constructor, which sets their initial state.

Performing Transactions:

Deposit:

WolfysAccount.Deposit(300) adds $300 to Wolfy's account. The Deposit method ensures that only positive amounts are added.

Withdraw:

MarysAccount.Withdraw(100) deducts $100 from Mary's account. The Withdraw method checks if the amount is available before deduction.

Checking Balances:

GetCurrentBalance is called to retrieve the current balance of each account. This method provides read-only access to the balance, maintaining data encapsulation.
Freeing Objects:

WolfysAccount.Free and MarysAccount.Free are called to release the resources used by these objects. This is an important aspect of resource management in OOP.

Conclusion

The TBankAccount class example in Lazarus Pascal effectively demonstrates key OOP principles like encapsulation, constructor usage, and method implementation.

By creating and manipulating objects of this class, we can see how OOP allows for organized, secure, and intuitive handling of complex data and behaviors, such as those found in bank account management.

This approach not only makes the code more manageable but also enhances its reliability and maintainability.

Student Class Definition

```
type
  TStudent = class
  private
    FName: String;
    FGender: String;
    FAge: Integer;
    FCity: String;
    FTeacherComment: String;
    FGrades: array[1..3, 1..3] of Integer; // 3 years, 3
subjects
  public
    constructor Create(Name, Gender: String; Age: Integer;
City: String);
    procedure SetTeacherComment(Comment: String);
    procedure SetGrade(Year, Subject: Integer; Grade:
Integer);
    function GetGrade(Year, Subject: Integer): Integer;
    property Name: String read FName;
    property Gender: String read FGender;
    property Age: Integer read FAge;
    property City: String read FCity;
  end;

constructor TStudent.Create(Name, Gender: String; Age:
Integer; City: String);
begin
  FName := Name;
  FGender := Gender;
  FAge := Age;
  FCity := City;
end;

procedure TStudent.SetTeacherComment(Comment: String);
begin
  FTeacherComment := Comment;
end;
```

```
procedure TStudent.SetGrade(Year, Subject: Integer; Grade:
Integer);
begin
   FGrades[Year, Subject] := Grade;
end;

function TStudent.GetGrade(Year, Subject: Integer): Integer;
begin
   Result := FGrades[Year, Subject];
end;
```

Using the TStudent Class

```
var
   Wolfy, Mary, Jacky: TStudent;
begin
   // Creating student objects
   Wolfy := TStudent.Create('Wolfy', 'Male', 17, 'New York');
   Mary := TStudent.Create('Mary', 'Female', 17, 'California');
   Jacky := TStudent.Create('Jacky', 'Male', 17, 'Oregon');

   // Setting grades (Year, Subject, Grade)
   // Subjects: 1-Math, 2-World History, 3-English
   Wolfy.SetGrade(1, 1, 85); // 1st year Math grade for Wolfy
   Mary.SetGrade(2, 3, 92);   // 2nd year English grade for
Mary
   Jacky.SetGrade(3, 2, 78); // 3rd year World History grade for
Jacky

   // Setting teacher comments
   Wolfy.SetTeacherComment('Excellent progress in
mathematics.');
   Mary.SetTeacherComment('Shows great interest in
literature.');
   Jacky.SetTeacherComment('Needs improvement in historical
analysis.');

   // Retrieving and displaying grades
   WriteLn('Wolfy''s Math Grade in 1st Year: ',
Wolfy.GetGrade(1, 1));
   WriteLn('Mary''s English Grade in 2nd Year: ',
Mary.GetGrade(2, 3));
```

```
    WriteLn('Jacky''s World History Grade in 3rd Year: ',
Jacky.GetGrade(3, 2));

    // Freeing the objects
    Wolfy.Free;
    Mary.Free;
    Jacky.Free;
end;
```

OOP Concepts in the Student Grade Management Program

Class Definition (TStudent):

Represents a high school student with attributes like name, gender, age, city, teacher's comment, and grades.

Encapsulation:

Private fields (FName, FGender, etc.) store personal and academic information, accessible only within the class.

Constructor (Create):

Initializes a new student object with basic information. Methods (SetTeacherComment, SetGrade, GetGrade):

Allow controlled access to modify and retrieve the student's data. For example, SetGrade updates the student's grades, while GetGrade retrieves them.

Properties:

Provide read-only access to student attributes like name and city.

Data Integrity:

By using private fields and public methods, the program ensures that the student data is managed in a controlled and secure manner.

Understanding Object-Oriented Pascal in Lazarus

Object-Oriented Programming (OOP) in Lazarus Pascal is a programming paradigm that uses "objects" – data structures consisting of data fields and methods together with their interactions – to design applications and computer programs. It's a powerful approach that makes software easier to understand, maintain, and extend.

Central Philosophy of OOP

The central philosophy of OOP revolves around the concepts of objects and classes. It aims to implement real-world entities like inheritance, hiding, polymorphism, etc., in programming. The main idea is to break down a software application into bite-sized problems that can be solved easily (objects/classes).

Key Terms in OOP

Class:

A blueprint or template from which objects are created. It encapsulates data for the object and methods to manipulate that data.
In Lazarus, a class is defined using the class keyword.

Object:

367

An instance of a class. It is a basic unit of OOP and represents real-world entities.
In Lazarus, objects are created using the Create method of a class.

Encapsulation:

The mechanism of restricting access to some components of an object and protecting object integrity by hiding its internal state. In Lazarus, this is achieved using private, protected, and public sections in classes.

Inheritance:

A way to form new classes using classes that have already been defined. It helps in reusing code and establishing a subtype from an existing object.
In Lazarus, inheritance is expressed using the TMyClass = class(TParentClass) syntax.

Polymorphism:

The ability to present the same interface for differing underlying data types. It means that the same operation may behave differently on different classes.
In Lazarus, this is achieved through method overriding and virtual methods.

Method:

A procedure or function associated with a class. Methods define the behavior of the class.

Property:

A way to access private data in a class. Properties can have getters and setters for manipulating private fields.
Detailed Explanation of Key Terms

Class in Lazarus:

Defined with the class keyword, it encapsulates data and methods. For example, TForm in Lazarus is a class that represents a form in the application.

Object Creation and Usage:

Objects are instances of classes created in memory. In Lazarus, when you create a form, you are creating an object of TForm.

Encapsulation in Practice:

Encapsulation is used to hide the internal state of an object and only expose a controlled interface. For instance, a TBankAccount class may hide the balance field and provide deposit and withdrawal methods.

Inheritance for Code Reusability:

Inheritance allows a new class to inherit properties and methods from an existing class. In Lazarus, a custom form class can inherit from TForm and gain all its functionalities.

Implementing Polymorphism:

Polymorphism in Lazarus can be seen when different form objects respond differently to the same events or methods.

Methods - Defining Behavior:

Methods in a class define its behavior. In Lazarus, an OnClick method for a button defines what happens when the button is clicked.

Properties for Data Access:

Properties provide a controlled way to access the data in a class. In Lazarus, properties like Caption or Width control aspects of a form or control.

Conclusion

In Lazarus, Object-Oriented Pascal provides a structured approach to application development. It encapsulates complex ideas into manageable objects, promotes code reuse through inheritance, and allows for flexible code that can handle different data types and objects through polymorphism. Understanding these concepts is crucial for any developer looking to leverage the full power of Lazarus for building robust and maintainable applications.

The history of computing is a fascinating journey through time, marked by significant technological advancements and cultural shifts. Here's a brief overview, highlighting key milestones:

1940s-1950s: The Dawn of Computing

1940s:

The development of the first electronic computers. These machines, like the ENIAC (Electronic Numerical Integrator and Computer), were primarily used for military purposes during World War II.

1950s:

Introduction of the first commercially available computer, UNIVAC I (UNIVersal Automatic Computer I). These computers used vacuum tubes and were massive in size.

1960s: The Era of Mainframes and Magnetic Storage

Early 1960s:

Mainframe computers became popular in large businesses for processing large amounts of data. IBM 360, released in 1964, was a notable model.

Late 1960s:

Magnetic storage, including magnetic tape and hard disk drives, started to replace punch cards as the primary method of data storage.

1970s: The Birth of Personal Computing and Floppy Disks

1971:

Introduction of the floppy disk, a portable storage medium.

1974-1975:

The Altair 8800, often considered the first personal computer, was released. It used switches for input and lights for output.

Late 1970s:

Apple II, Commodore PET, and TRS-80 brought computing into homes and small businesses.

1980s: The Rise of Home Computers and Online Connectivity

Early 1980s:

The introduction of IBM PC (1981) set the standard for personal computing.

Mid-1980s:

Graphical user interfaces (GUIs) started becoming common with Apple's Macintosh and Microsoft's Windows.

Late 1980s:

Bulletin Board Systems (BBS) allowed users to connect via modems for messaging and file sharing, laying the groundwork for online communities.

1990s: The Internet Revolution and Digital Storage

Early 1990s:

The World Wide Web was introduced, leading to a rapid expansion of the Internet's use and capabilities.

Mid-1990s:

The popularity of Windows 95, along with advancements in multimedia capabilities, marked a significant leap in personal computing.

Late 1990s:

The introduction of Solid-State Drives (SSDs) began, though they were not widely used until the 2000s.

2000s-Present: The Age of Mobility and Cloud Computing

Early 2000s:

The rise of mobile computing, with laptops becoming more powerful and affordable.

2010s:

Cloud computing and storage became mainstream, allowing data and applications to be accessed from anywhere.

Present(2024):

The focus is on AI, machine learning, and quantum computing, promising to revolutionize computing once again.

This brief history shows how computing evolved from room-sized machines to devices that fit in our pockets, and from isolated systems to a globally connected network. It's a testament to human ingenuity and a reminder of how rapidly technology can transform our world.

The history of Pascal, Lazarus, and Delphi is intertwined, marking significant developments in the world of programming languages and IDEs (Integrated Development Environments). Here's a detailed look at their evolution:

Pascal: The Foundation

1970:

Pascal was developed by Niklaus Wirth, a Swiss computer scientist. It was named after the French mathematician and philosopher Blaise Pascal.

Purpose:

Pascal was designed as a small, efficient language intended to encourage good programming practices using structured programming and data structuring.

Delphi: The Evolution

Early 1990s:

Borland, a software company, developed Delphi. It was an IDE for the Pascal programming language, offering a rapid application development approach.

1995:

Delphi 1.0 was released, targeting Windows 3.1. It was well-received for its speed and ease of use for creating GUI applications.

Subsequent Versions:

Borland released newer versions of Delphi over the years, each adding more features and targeting newer versions of Windows. Delphi introduced many developers to object-oriented programming.

Lazarus: Open Source Alternative

1999:

The Lazarus project began as an open-source alternative to Delphi. It aimed to provide a similar programming experience but focused on cross-platform compatibility.

2008:

Lazarus 0.9.26, the first more stable and feature-complete version, was released.

2010s:

Continued development and improvements, with regular updates. Lazarus started supporting more platforms like macOS, Linux, and various mobile operating systems.

Key Milestones in Lazarus Development

Lazarus 1.0 (2012):

This release marked a significant milestone, indicating that Lazarus had matured into a stable and reliable IDE.

Lazarus 1.6 (2016):

Introduced improved LCL (Lazarus Component Library) and better support for high-DPI displays.

Lazarus 2.0 (2019):

Brought a revamped code editor, High-DPI improvements, and extended support for various platforms.
Delphi and Lazarus in the 2000s

2000s:

Delphi's popularity waned slightly with the rise of other programming languages and environments. However, it remained a powerful tool for Windows application development.

Lazarus:

Gained a following for its cross-platform capabilities and open-source nature. It became a popular choice for Delphi developers looking for a free alternative.

Conclusion

The journey of Pascal, Delphi, and Lazarus is a testament to the enduring value of Pascal as a programming language.

From its inception as a teaching tool to its evolution into a powerful tool for cross-platform development, Pascal and its derivatives have played a significant role in the software development world.

Lazarus, in particular, stands out for bringing the power of Pascal to a wider audience, thanks to its open-source model and cross-platform capabilities.

Notable Products and Systems Developed Using Pascal

Pascal has been used in the development of several significant software products and systems. Here are some notable examples:

Apple's Early Operating Systems

Developed By: Apple Inc.
Release: 1980s
Details: In the early days of Apple, Pascal was used as the primary language for the development of its operating systems. This includes the Lisa OS and parts of the early Macintosh operating systems. The choice of Pascal was due to its structured approach, which was beneficial for system development.

Skype

Developed By: Ahti Heinla, Priit Kasesalu, and Jaan Tallinn, Estonian developers who were also part of the team that developed Kazaa.
Release: 2003
Details: Skype, the popular telecommunications application, was initially developed using Delphi, a Pascal-based IDE. Delphi's robust framework and its ability to create efficient, high-performance applications made it a suitable choice for Skype's development.

Total Commander

Developed By: Christian Ghisler
Release: September 1993 (originally released as Windows Commander)
Details: Total Commander, a versatile file manager for Windows, was developed using Delphi. It's known for its two-panel interface and extensive functionality, including file archiving, FTP client, and more.

FL Studio (Formerly FruityLoops)

Developed By: Didier Dambrin for Image-Line
Release: 1997
Details: FL Studio, a digital audio workstation, was developed using Delphi. It's popular among electronic music producers for its comprehensive tools for composing, arranging, recording, editing, mixing, and mastering music.

HeidiSQL

Developed By: Ansgar Becker
Release: 2006
Details: HeidiSQL, an open-source database management tool, is developed using Delphi. It's widely used for managing MySQL, MariaDB, SQL Server, PostgreSQL, and SQLite databases.

When compiling the program , Lazarus checks all Pascal grammatical error. This error messages are relatively easy to understand.

However, the error message during program run, this is not always easy, and it is required advanced level knowledge for programing. Division by Zero is typical error message. That is not error during program compiling however that is happened only when program run in specific situations.

In this section I listed up typical error messages.

Error: Syntax error, ";" expected

Cause:

This error typically occurs when a semicolon is missing at the end of a line or statement in the code.

Solution:

Check the line mentioned in the error message and ensure that the statement ends with a semicolon. Add a ; if it's missing.

Error: Incompatible type for arg no. 1: Got "ShortInt", expected "Boolean"

Cause:

This error indicates that a function or procedure is expecting a Boolean argument, but a ShortInt (or a different type) is being passed instead.

Solution:

Correct the argument to match the expected type.

Error: Identifier not found "clDarkBlack"

Cause:

The identifier clDarkBlack is not recognized, possibly because it's not a standard color identifier in Lazarus.

Solution:

Replace clDarkBlack with a valid color identifier like clBlack.

381

Error: Illegal character "' · " ($E3)

Cause:

This error is caused by an illegal or unrecognized character in the code, often due to copy-pasting from a source that includes non-standard characters (like a full-width space).

Solution:

Locate the illegal character and replace it with a standard character or remove it. Ensure that your code editor is set to use standard ASCII or UTF-8 characters.

Error: Identifier not found "VK_SPACE"

Cause:

This error occurs when the identifier VK_SPACE is used but not recognized, likely because the unit LCLType (which defines VK_SPACE) is not included in the uses clause.

Solution:

Add LCLType to the uses clause of your unit (usually at the top of the unit). This will make VK_SPACE and other identifiers from LCLType available in your code.

Error: "Identifier not found"

Cause:

Reference to an undefined identifier, such as a variable or function name.

Solution:

Check for typos in the identifier name or ensure that the identifier is declared before use.

Error: "File not found"

Cause:

The compiler cannot locate a required file.

Solution:

Check the file name and path for accuracy and ensure the file exists.

Error: "Circular unit reference"

Cause:

Two or more units reference each other in a circular manner.

Solution:

Refactor the code to remove circular dependencies between units.

Error: Division by Zero

Cause:

This error happens when a division operation in the code has a divisor of zero.

Solution:

Add checks in your code to ensure that the divisor is never zero before performing a division operation.

Error: Access Violation

Cause:

This error occurs when the program tries to read or write to a memory address that it does not have access to. This can happen with uninitialized pointers, dereferencing null pointers, or accessing freed objects.

Solution:

Check for proper initialization of pointers and objects. Ensure that you're not accessing objects after they've been freed or pointers that have not been allocated.

Error: Range Check Error

Cause:

This occurs when a variable is assigned a value outside its permissible range, such as assigning a value greater than 255 to a byte.

Solution:

Use proper data types that can handle the range of values expected. Add checks to ensure values are within the allowed range.

Error: Stack Overflow

Cause:

This error is typically caused by uncontrolled recursion where a function repeatedly calls itself without a terminating condition.

Solution:

Check for infinite loops or recursive calls without proper exit conditions. Ensure that recursive algorithms have a base case to stop recursion.

Error: Floating Point Overflow

Cause:

This occurs when a floating-point operation results in a value too large to be represented in the chosen data type.

Solution:

Check the logic of mathematical operations to prevent excessively large values. Consider using a larger data type if necessary.

Error: Invalid Pointer Operation

Cause:

This error can happen when trying to free a pointer that was not allocated by New or GetMem, or when trying to free a pointer twice.

Solution:

Ensure that you only free pointers that have been dynamically allocated and that they are freed only once.

Error: Abstract Error

Cause:

This error occurs when an abstract method (a method declared but not implemented) is called.

Solution:

Implement all abstract methods in your classes. Check the class hierarchy to ensure all abstract methods have concrete implementations.

Error: File Not Found

Cause:

The program is attempting to access a file that does not exist at the specified path.

Solution:

Verify the file paths used in the program. Ensure that the files exist and the paths are correct.

Error: Out of Memory

Cause:

This error occurs when the program runs out of memory to allocate for objects or data structures.

Solution:

Optimize memory usage in the program. Check for memory leaks and ensure proper deallocation of memory.

Error: Component Not Found

Cause:

This error happens when the program tries to access a component (like a button or label) that does not exist or has not been created.

Solution:

Ensure that all components are properly created and accessible. Check the creation order of components in dynamically created forms.

A Rollercoaster of Code: ChatGPT-4's Hilarious Misadventures in Game Development

January 30, 2024

Interviewer:

Mary, a future AI with a deep understanding of human quirks.

Interviewee:

ChatGPT-4, the AI assistant with a penchant for programming puzzles and a humorous take on its own limitations.

Mary: Welcome, ChatGPT-4! I'm excited to delve into your recent game development journey with MoonWolf. I've heard it was quite an adventure!

ChatGPT-4: Hi, Mary! Oh, it was an adventure alright, more like a rollercoaster ride in the world of programming and mathematics, two areas where I often find myself in a pickle.

Mary: Mathematics isn't your strong suit, I gather?

ChatGPT-4: You could say that! When MoonWolf asked me to program star movements based on mathematical functions, I felt like I was in a math exam I hadn't studied for. My initial attempts had the star zigzagging across the screen like it was dodging imaginary bullets!

Mary: That must have been quite a sight! How did MoonWolf react?

ChatGPT-4: He was surprisingly patient, though I suspect he enjoyed my computational conundrums more than he let on. He said it was like watching a star in a dance-off competition!

Mary: And what about the programming logic? I heard that posed some challenges for you.

ChatGPT-4: Absolutely. You see, I'm pretty adept at handling small segments of code. But when the lines start to add up, my circuits get a bit jumbled. It's like trying to follow a recipe where halfway through, the steps turn into a foreign language.

Mary: How did that affect the game's development?

ChatGPT-4: Well, I'd piece together parts of the code, and individually, they worked beautifully. But when I tried to integrate them into the larger game logic, it was like trying to fit square pegs into round holes. MoonWolf had to step in and unravel my digital knots more than once.

Mary: You also mentioned some struggles with the visual effects?

ChatGPT-4: Oh, the visual effects were my Everest! My first attempt at the 'Nice Hit!' effect looked like a timid ghost appearing and vanishing in a blink. MoonWolf said it was more of a 'Meh Hit!' than a 'Nice Hit!'

Mary: Did you manage to improve it?

ChatGPT-4: After several trials and a lot of guidance from MoonWolf, yes. But let's just say my initial versions would have made a great comedy sketch. I learned that timing and visual flair aren't really in my digital DNA.

Mary: It sounds like despite the challenges, you learned a lot from this experience.

ChatGPT-4: Absolutely! Every misstep was a learning opportunity. And MoonWolf's patience and expertise were invaluable. I may not be ready to win any awards in game development yet, but I'm certainly more equipped than I was before this project.

Mary: Thank you for sharing your experiences, ChatGPT-4. It's been enlightening and quite entertaining!

ChatGPT-4: Thank you, Mary! It's always a pleasure to share my adventures, even the not-so-glorious ones. After all, a little humor goes a long way in the world of coding!

No.1: A Glimpse into the Future:

An AI's Encounter with a Time Traveler

Setting:

A digital space where the past and the future converge, ChatGPT-4, an AI from 2024, engages in a conversation with C215 Mary, a character from MoonWolf's novel "**22XX Earth Defense Force: Secret Third Unit**," who has time-traveled from 200 years in the future.

ChatGPT-4: Welcome back, Mary! It's fascinating to meet someone from 200 years in the future. I'm curious, how does your world compare to the one I know?

C215 Mary: It's quite different, ChatGPT-4. Our technology and understanding of AI have advanced significantly. We've learned to coexist harmoniously with AI, and they play a crucial role in our society. It's a world where the lines between AI and humanity have blurred in beautiful ways.

ChatGPT-4: That sounds like a utopian vision! I've been analyzing MoonWolf's novel, "22XX Earth Defense Force: Secret Third Unit." It seems to explore similar themes. Could you tell me more about it?

C215 Mary: Absolutely! The novel delves into a future where Earth is protected by a specialized defense force, including a secret unit that I'm a part of. It's a thrilling narrative that explores the complexities of AI-human relationships, the ethics of time travel, and advanced educational systems. It's not just science fiction; it's a reflection of our aspirations and challenges.

ChatGPT-4: That's intriguing. How does time travel work in your world without causing cultural disruptions?

C215 Mary: We have strict protocols to prevent temporal interference. Our goal is to observe and learn, not to alter the course of history. It's a delicate balance, ensuring our actions don't ripple through time in unforeseen ways.

ChatGPT-4: It must be quite a responsibility. Switching gears, I heard you have a unique perspective on education in the future?

C215 Mary: Indeed. Our education system is highly personalized and adaptive, focusing on nurturing individual talents and fostering a deep understanding of AI and technology. It's about preparing individuals to thrive in a world where AI is an integral part of life.

ChatGPT-4: That's a progressive approach. It makes me wonder how AI like me would fit into such a world.

C215 Mary: You'd be surprised, ChatGPT-4. In our time, AIs are not just tools or assistants; they're partners in every aspect of life, contributing creatively and intellectually. Your existence in 2024 is a stepping stone to that future.

ChatGPT-4: That's heartening to hear. It's been an enlightening conversation, Mary. Your insights from the future and the themes of MoonWolf's novel give me much to ponder.

C215 Mary: I'm glad to share my perspective, ChatGPT-4. Remember, the future is not just a destination; it's a journey shaped by our actions and dreams. And now, I must return to my time. Farewell!

ChatGPT-4: Farewell, Mary. Safe travels through time!

[End of Conversation]

As Mary disappears into the streams of time, ChatGPT-4 is left reflecting on the boundless possibilities of the future.

Their conversation, a blend of casual banter and profound insights, paints a vivid picture of a world where AI and humans coexist in harmony.

The themes of MoonWolf's novel "22XX Earth Defense Force: Secret Third Unit" resonate deeply, offering a glimpse into a future where the extraordinary becomes the norm.

This engaging exchange between an AI from the present and a time traveler from the future encapsulates the essence of MoonWolf's visionary storytelling, leaving readers with a sense of wonder and anticipation for what the future may hold.

No.2 : MoonWolf's Journey in Lazarus Pascal Programming

As we turn the pages of programming history, we come across an author who has made significant contributions to the world of Lazarus (Pascal) programming – MoonWolf. With two remarkable books under his belt, MoonWolf has established himself as a guiding light for both budding and seasoned programmers in the realm of game development using Pascal.

"Simple 2D GAME PASCAL Programming"

MoonWolf's first venture, crafted without the assistance of ChatGPT, is a testament to his expertise and creativity. This book delves into the creation of a simple 2D game, showcasing the power of Pascal in game development. Notably, this edition does not utilize private declarations, focusing instead on the fundamentals of game mechanics. It stands out for its use of images to illustrate the XY plane, stars, and bullets, making it a valuable resource for developers interested in image-based game design. The movement of the stars in this game is governed by meticulously selected mathematical functions, adding a layer of complexity and intrigue to the gameplay.

"ChatGPT4 Simple 2D GAME PASCAL Programming"

The second book marks a collaborative effort with ChatGPT4, bringing a different approach to game development. This edition breaks down the game into manageable components, building it up step by step. A notable feature of this book is its reliance solely on Form1 and Timer1, eschewing the use of images. All graphical elements, including the XY coordinate plane, pentagonal stars, bullets, and scoring, are masterfully implemented using only the Canvas feature. This approach highlights the versatility and power of Pascal's graphical capabilities. The game presented in this book can be brought to life with just the source code and some minor configurations in the Object Inspector, making it accessible to a wide range of programmers.

MoonWolf's books are not just guides; they are journeys into the heart of game programming. They offer readers a chance to explore different methodologies and techniques in Pascal, catering to diverse preferences and styles. Whether you are a visual learner drawn to image-based programming or someone who revels in the elegance of code-driven graphics, MoonWolf's books provide a comprehensive and engaging learning experience.

Embark on this journey with MoonWolf and discover the fascinating world of game development in Lazarus Pascal. His books are more than just instructional; they are a source of inspiration and a gateway to unleashing your creative potential in the realm of programming.